Beth
Thank you
for the love +
support! Joshua 1:9

Praise for Ashlee Leppert and
The Hurricane Within

An outstanding read and a must-have on any shelf. Follow this hero through harrowing Coast Guard search and rescue missions while managing an array of stressors impacting her health. The gripping story about the girl next door grabs your attention as she navigates personally and professionally the storms of life. Follow her through the demands and dangers U.S. Coast Guard women and men routinely confront, and how faith propelled her through her darkest times. A true success story about overcoming obstacles and shinning during her greatest moments as a U.S. Coast Guard aviator.

—Broderick W. Johnson,
United States Coast Guard (ret.)
12th Enlisted Ancient Albatross

The Hurricane Within shows the selflessness and courage required of Ashlee and all members of the U.S. Coast Guard to keep Americans safe. Ashlee's accounts of the heroic rescues she participated in during Hurricane Harvey make you feel like you are flying right alongside her.

—Scott DeLuzio, Army veteran,
author of *Surviving Son*,
and host of Drive On Podcast

Ms. Ashlee Leppert (U.S. Coast Guard Petty Officer Second Class) was highly recommended to me as a guest speaker to the Destin FL Military Affairs Council (MAC). She graciously agreed to speak and the result was a standing ovation from that audience. Her presentation was polished and engaging. She told of the challenging life situations that led to her enlistment in the United States Coast Guard and then about achieving her career goals as a flight mechanic and as a flight mechanic instructor. Her adventures in performing her duties were remarkable and captivating. Her confident, inspirational performance in front of the audience created exactly the atmosphere I was hoping for and her story touched our hearts as well. I greatly recommend her as a guest speaker to any audience.

—Kim M. Wintner, Col. USAF (ret.)
Chairman, Destin MAC, Vice Chairman, Emerald Coast MAC; Board Member, Mid Bay Bridge Authority
(by Fla. Gov. appt.)

I have to say that despite working on over 300 books in my career Ashlee Leppert's *The Hurricane Within* was both surprising, inspirational, memorable, and very much something I remained eager to read. Her story is presented like an engaging novel, in fact I have told others about much of it, which from my view is a great sign! I was engaged and rooting for her throughout, especially as the stakes were raised and at the end (no spoilers!). Even today I am left with a sense of wonder at all she went through, what she has done with her experience (now an inspirational speaker), and how God works. Bravo! A must-read!

—Rodney Miles, Editor

The Hurricane Within

The Hurricane Within

Hurricane Harvey through the eyes of a Coast Guard flight mechanic. Her story of perseverance, resilience and trusting in God's plan.

Ashlee Leppert

United States Coast Guard Air Medal Recipient

Copyright © 2019 by Ashlee Leppert
All rights reserved.
Published by Mandi Pants Press

No part of this book may be reproduced in any manner without written permission except in the case of brief quotations embodied in critical articles and reviews.

Although the author and publisher have made every effort to ensure that the information in this book was correct at press time, the author and publisher do not assume and hereby disclaim any liability to any party for any loss, damage, or disruption caused by errors or omissions, whether such errors or omissions result from negligence, accident, or any other cause.

For information about special discounts for bulk purchases or author interviews, appearances, and speaking engagements please contact:

Ashlee Leppert
c/o Mandi Pants Press
www.AshleeLeppert.com

First Edition

Edited by Katherine O'Nale and Erin McPhail
Final editing, cover, jacket, book and page design by Rodney Miles, www.RodneyMiles.com
All images © the author unless noted.

My Hurricane Flight Crews

Thanks for keeping me safe. Thanks for keeping me focused.

LCDR Larry Santos

LT Andrew Breen

AST2 Robert Hovey

LT Drake Thornton

LT Ryan O'Neill

AST3 Nathan Feske-Wood

LT John Briggs

LT Gregory Bukata

AST2 Troy Ramsdell

This is a story about fearless and unrelenting strength—the mental strength that carries us through the small battles we face daily as we compartmentalize the silent victories; the physical strength that evolves day after day, even when your own health is the enemy. This is my story, my unseen internal war; all the while smiling in the face of adversity and peering into the eyes of the helpless.

*Heavenly Father, I pray that this is Your light
and that all the Glory be to You.*

Contents

Part One: Coasties 1

[1] Another Day 2

[2] A Very Real Fact 5

[3] Like it Never Happened 10

[4] Duty 15

[5] Off the Ground 30

[6] New Orleans 42

[7] The Specialists 57

[8] Something Bigger 71

[9] The Beach 84

Part Two: Hurricane 91

[10] Briefing 92

[11] Rescue 98

[12] Storm Born 114

[13] My New Crew 122

[14] The Cross 129

[15] The Basket 137

[16] Water Intrusion 145

[17] My Final Hoist 152

[18] One More Rescue	164

Epilogue	167
Afterword	177
About the Author	183
Speaking	184
Acknowledgements	185
Learn More	188

Part One:
Coasties

[1] Another Day

"My mission in life is to not merely survive, but to thrive; and to do so with some passion, some compassion, some humor, and some style."

—Maya Angelou

O600. MY PHONE started to vibrate and sing the familiar tune that means it's time to wake up and start another day. I chose this ringtone because it's cheerful and I wanted to start every day the way I'm supposed to—as a gift from God. But this ringtone has pulled me out of a deep sleep a few too many times and it doesn't seem so cheerful anymore. It will need to be changed soon. I opened my eyes and lazily looked around my room. My eyes couldn't seem to focus out of this odd double vision and everything in the room seemed hazy. My black lab, Mandi, looked like a big black fuzzy shadow that stretched out to fill up most of the bed. She's a big girl. With a soft wag of the tail, she put her belly up in the air for her morning scratches. She has been the one constant in my chaotic world, and my best friend. The house was quieter and my habits had been thrown into disarray. Everything I had planned for my future was suddenly unsure with the upcoming and inevitable military move to a new duty station. I liked having a general idea of what to expect. I could plan and make decisions. Complete uncertainty can be so stressful.

After giving Mandi a few well-deserved belly scratches and kisses, I rolled out of bed and made it over to the mirror on my dresser. Double vision seemed to have become a new norm for me. My eyes still couldn't seem to focus but I could see the glow of my striking blond hair cascaded over my shoulders. I could just make out a rough outline of my body, my strong build. At 5'10, I'm taller than most women I know.

"Come on, girl! Time to come alive!" I called, both to myself and to Mandi Pants. "I don't have time for fatigue."

I've never cared much for any adage that suggests a woman should be seen and not heard. I preferred to be both. People took notice when I entered a room. I was the loud, boisterous, tall blonde with a larger-than-life personality. I would walk into a bar and crack a dirty joke as I passed by my friends to grab a drink. In social situations, I was usually greeted with a unanimous sense of "Ashlee's here! Now the party can start!" I've always been that way, and I've grown to love being that person, although at times I have envied those who are a bit more introverted. My personality was uninhibited. I laughed loudly at things I probably shouldn't have, I made friends with strangers, I was one hell of a dancer, and I loved being the life of the party.

In stark contrast, I could be calm and collective. I could go from "wild Ashlee" to a woman capable of making multiple split-second decisions in a fast-moving and dangerous environment. When responding to emergencies, my voice was steady and calm, my body moved in a swift and powerful manner, and my mind was clear. When it was time to do my job, everything in the world but my task on hand seemed to melt away. I suppose my personality was a bit dichotomous. I was hardwired with some sort of mental switch that I could turn on and off at will.

I poured myself a cup of coffee. The drink helped me kick-start my day. I took another look in the mirror. Everything came into focus. *About time*, I thought to myself. I pulled my hair back into a semi-neat bun, put on a touch of makeup, and slipped into the blue uniform I had been wearing for years. I swear, the uniform would develop wrinkles and creases no matter what you did to it.

I kissed Ms. Mandi Pants goodbye and mustered the energy and enthusiasm to face another day.

[2] A Very Real Fact

"Greater love has no one than this, that someone lay down his life for his friends."

—John 15:13

I PULLED INTO Coast Guard Air Station Detroit in time to watch one of the bright orange MH-65 "Dolphins" take off. Yes, I said *Coast Guard*. I often felt the need to emphasize that because few people seemed to hear about us or understand our mission. One of several things typically happened whenever I told someone I was in the Coast Guard. First, that person might laugh and call me a Puddle Pirate—a nickname given to Coasties by other military branches. There's a sense of playful jab that takes place between military, but a civilian has no business engaging in such name calling. Second, that person might point out, "But you're not six feet tall!" I would feign confusion at this because everyone thinks they are original when they told this joke. They follow up with, "So if your boat sinks you can walk to shore!" at which point I would extend to them my most sarcastic of laughs. Lastly, and perhaps most infuriating, I might get a long speech about how the Coast Guard isn't really a branch of the military.

Admittedly, the Coast Guard was very different from the other branches of the military. We had an entirely different mission, focused more on the safety and security on American soil instead of focusing on threats from abroad. Coasties didn't pretend to be war heroes—okay, some did, but the rest of us didn't like those guys, either.

We became the red-headed step-children of the military. We were quite accustomed to being dismissed as unimportant or inconsequential. Nobody should have to explain why their job is, in fact, worthy of some degree of admiration. People died doing what I did. Imagine yourself in the following scenario: A Coast Guard helicopter goes missing. The news of a crash ripples through the aviation community like a shock wave. The hangars go deathly silent as everyone sneaks away to text their friends who work at the station that lost the aircraft. Nothing gets done. You have plenty of work to do, but you can't seem to organize your thoughts. Some sit around and engage in mindless banter to distract from the palpable fear while we wait for news. They jump the instant someone's phone makes a noise. Everyone waits with baited-breath, hoping and praying that the message received was a good one. Coast Guard aviation is small and incredibly tight-knit. Nobody says it, but everyone thinks it. If there is a death, someone probably just lost a friend, and we've all lost a family member. With a rock in our gut, we wait to find out who. I can't imagine this happens in many other occupations.

The Hurricane Within

It had been a few hours since the helicopter stopped responding to radio hails. A few desperate suggestions as to why the helicopter lost communications were presented but have since been abandoned. The aircraft wouldn't have had enough fuel to keep flying this long. There's a difference between optimistic and unrealistic. Each crewmember carries a radio in their flight vest, a radio that transmits on channel 16, the emergency maritime channel that every boat on the water, civilian and otherwise, is required to monitor. It had been eerily silent.

The crew was dead.

A typical crew on a Coast Guard helicopter consists of a pilot, a copilot, a flight mechanic, and a rescue swimmer. Four souls. Within half a day, the community pinpoints the four people that have gone radio silent. It was time to accept the fact that your friend will never respond to that "are you ok?" text message. Everyone had been accounted for. You go home, pour a drink, and let out a few tears in silence. And that's it. You go back to work, you hop in the same helicopters and you perform the same missions. Every now and then you stop for a second when the news media releases their names, or you see a picture of the helicopter's shredded fuselage being craned out of the water. The news then announces that three of the crew members' bodies have been recovered. Your friend is still missing. They'll find his bloated body floating around more than a week later. Memories of your time together in training school will instantly surface, along with tears of devastation.

ASHLEE LEPPERT

Never Forgotten Helicopter Crew #6535

Now imagine biting your tongue and smiling when someone makes an off-handed comment that "the Coast Guard doesn't actually do anything," just days after attending a memorial service. It's enraging.

The very real fact of the matter is that I made the commitment to lay down my life, if need be, in service to my country and its citizens. I knowingly, and repeatedly, put myself into dangerous situations that could quickly end in disaster. But it was worth it. The passion I had for my mission far exceeded any concerns I had for my personal safety. There have been several times throughout my career when my life flashed before my eyes or I took off on a mission knowing I may not return.

It was my faith in my flight crews and, most importantly, my faith in God that filled me with a sense of peace and fearlessness.

My first flight ever in a HH-65B Dolphin Helicopter back in 2007.

[3] Like it Never Happened

"Not only that, but we rejoice in our sufferings, knowing that sufferings produce endurance, and endurance produces character, and character produces hope, and that hope does not put us to shame, because God's love has been poured into our hearts through the Holy Spirit who has been given to us."

—Romans 5:3-5

I ALMOST DIDN'T fulfill my dream of flying in Coast Guard helicopters. Back in 2009, I was halfway through Avionics Electrical Technician School when my days of drinking out as a young 22-year-old almost halted my dreams. I had just transferred into aviation training center Elizabeth City, N.C, from almost two years of being stationed on the beautiful island of Puerto Rico. As a young adult, I found myself thrust deep into the "work hard, party harder" lifestyle. The Medalla beer and Bacardi cocktails flowed like water. Just upon leaving the island for training, my co-workers on the hanger deck would warn me, "Now Ash, you're going back to the mainland where this isn't the lifestyle there. So be careful." I heard that warning and tried to heed it.

After one long night out drinking to relieve our brains from the constant study and learning mode, I got pulled over and charged with a DWI. I was pulled over and given a field sobriety test. I failed, *miserably*. Of course in the moment I blamed my recent ankle injury on my terrible balance and inability to walk straight. The breathalyzer instantly revealed otherwise. My ankle wasn't the culprit, rather the double-vodka Red Bulls flowing through my veins. I was polite and compliant fully knowing the mistake I had made. The officer who arrested me was a very kind man and even took the handcuffs off me as we drove back to base where he dropped me off at the front gate. We shared a cigarette as I cried my tears of remorse. The feelings of internal disgust flowed through my veins right alongside the potent level of vodka. I knew he had a job to do and didn't blame him. Now I had a job to do—pay my debt to my service and society and get back to aviation training school as soon as possible.

I was beyond devastated and disappointed in myself but even more thankful I didn't hurt anyone. The days and months that followed were the true test of my character. I was kicked out of training and sent to a small boat station in St. Inigoes, Maryland, basically in the middle of nowhere. I was told that I had to wait a year before re-entering training again. I worked tirelessly to earn my respect and reputation back. Initially the crew wasn't so welcoming. And could I blame them? I was the "fuck up" who got kicked out of training. I made it my mission to prove otherwise. I wasn't going to let my youthfully naïve mistake dictate my life.

As a non-rate, I was in charge of the lowest on the totem pole type jobs—mess-cooking, boat checks, sounding the fuel, painting, and any task your chain of command asked of you. For the next six months or so I worked my butt off to get every qualification possible. I wanted to be an asset and prove my worth to the unit. Soon everyone welcomed me with open arms. It was quite refreshing to have them see the real me. It was because of great mentorship from that boat unit and chiefs like Christopher Harward that I was mentally prepared to return to the training center and achieve the goal I had set off to complete over a year earlier.

Christopher Harward was not only the commanding officer (CO) at my new duty station but he was a kind-hearted, easily approachable guy who smiled and joked regardless of the authority of his position. I immediately felt comfortable in his presence. He saw through my DWI mistake. He felt like my own Mr. Miyagi (from the movie, *Karate Kid*), teaching me simple life lessons that would ultimately help me win the fight. He didn't know it then, but my days spent at his unit were made impactful by his leadership. He had faith in me even when I didn't have faith in myself.

Looking back on these early years, a lot of my actions involving drinking in excess and being a wild child made sense. When I was 19 or so, my innocence was shattered when I was sexually assaulted. This was only a few short months before I entered boot camp with my dearest friend Nicole and begin a career I was so excited about. I didn't really know what to do so I just bundled that incident up and tucked it real deep into the depths of my soul. There is no perfect, outlined, nice and neat way on how to deal with such trauma. For me, avoidance made it easy. If I pretended it didn't happen then just maybe I would eventually *forget this nightmare*, right?

I was scared of disrupting my opportunity to serve my country knowing I was going to boot camp only a few short months later. Avoidance for me looked like a lot of drinking and making a joke out of sex. By making a joke of it, deep in my subconscious it would minimize the severity of what happened to me. It's crazy how the brain copes. Laugh about it and it becomes insignificant. This method helped me forget for a while. I didn't mention anything then and was reluctant to do so now because I never wanted to be looked at like a victim. But just like any form of trauma, if not dealt with appropriately, it will eventually come back to haunt you.

I kept on smiling and living as though it never happened.

Ashlee Leppert

USCG Boot Camp graduation with Nicole Finley, Cape May New Jersey, October 5, 2005.

[4] Duty

"Once you have tasted flight, you will forever walk the earth with your eyes turned skyward, for there you have been, and there you will always long to return."

—Leonardo Di Vinci

I WAS STANDING Flight Mechanic duty. For the next 24 hours, I would be one of four crewmembers to jump into the helicopter and respond to emergencies. Our operations for the next two weeks would be taking place out of Air Facility Muskegon, Michigan. It was Air Station Detroit's second home in the summer months because of the busy boating season on the Great Lakes.

I loved standing duty.

In the Coast Guard, enlisted aviators were also fixers and flyers. There wasn't a great deal of specialization because the manpower simply didn't exist. When I wasn't flying, I was turning wrenches on the aircraft or I was performing routine inspections and initiating repairs on any discrepancies I might find. My official job title was Avionics Electrical Technician, so I would also conduct electrical troubleshooting or look into issues with communication and navigation equipment. On occasion, I would get put on a heavy maintenance team that pulled the engines and the main gearbox, which was the powerhouse of the aircraft. Aside from working on the aircraft, I was also expected to help maintain the fuel farm, fix ground support equipment, and work in the battery shop. There was always a ton of work to do, and never enough people to do it.

Standing duty almost felt like a break. While on duty, we wore a flight suit instead of the standard blue operational dress uniforms (ODUs). While on duty, you might have to drop everything and take off on a case without a moment's notice and you didn't want to be elbows-deep in the gearbox when it happened. Some Coastie's would argue that the downfall of standing duty was the likelihood of being woken up in the middle of the night and having to fly until sunrise. But for me, those were the nights that I lived for. I certainly didn't choose to work in Coast Guard aviation with simple dreams of applying anti-corrosive compound to aircraft parts day-in and day-out. I wanted to be out where the action was.

It was almost 1500, which was when oncoming duty takes over. As I made my way across the hangar towards the Operations Center for the oncoming duty brief, one of my colleagues yelled across the hangar, "Ashlee! You coming to softball on Thursday?"

"You know it!" I yelled back. "Ya'll can't win without me!" I joked.

Senior Chief poked his head around a corner upon hearing my voice. "Ashlee!" he yelled. "I need your dream sheet for your next duty station."

"I'll get it to you after my brief, Senior Chief."

"There she is!" Will Werner yelled good-naturedly from the top of the helicopter. Will Werner was a "salty" second class—"salty" meaning he had many years of experience and was the resident expert in all things mechanical. His bleach blonde hair could be used as an SOS if need be, and his mouth was always gleaming vividly with a huge smile. I worked nights with him. He taught me about engines, hydraulics, and most importantly about Tribal Seeds and Rebelution, two of his favorite bands.

He had a blade pin in one hand and grease in the other. "Just in time for us to wrap up our work!" He smirked and pressed the blade pin back into place.

"I don't want to hear it!" I teased back. "You know I did all of your paperwork and tools and trash!"

I escaped the hangar and rounded the corner into the operations center. The walls of the operations center were adorned with aviation charts, radio frequencies and important phone numbers. I was a few minutes early to the brief, but my two pilots and my rescue swimmer were already there.

"I'm here!" I announced as I enter the room.

"Yeah, because we definitely couldn't hear you coming," teased Nate Feske. *Good ole Nate Feske* was a true Texan through and through. His fun and quirky personality melded perfectly with mine and we soon became the best of pals. We had a lot of fun both at work and around town. He quickly became a guy I trusted both in and out of the helicopter. He was, and still is one of my greatest friends. Little did I know that we would not only save lives as a helicopter crew in Michigan together, but again in Houston for Hurricane Harvey response. Being a hero runs in his genes. His father was one of the first rescue swimmers to graduate for the Coast Guard Rescue Swimmer Program. I flew with the elite.

I leaned in close to him and said in a hushed voice, "You just remember who's controlling that cable the next time you're dangling from that helicopter."

With a wink from me, he chuckled and shook his head.

"Hi guys! Let's get started," said the pilot, Lt. Donaldson. I always enjoyed standing duty with this pilot. While she was sweet as could be, she was bold as they came and wouldn't let anyone push her around. "Today our flight mechanic is Ashlee, our swimmer is Nate, the copilot is LT Tritchler, and I am the pilot in command." She informed us of any TFR's and Notam's in our area of operations. TFR's were *temporary flight restrictions* and Notam's were issued to inform aviators of possible flight hazards. Most importantly, we discussed weather. The easiest way to get yourself into a bad situation was to not know what you're flying into. "Any questions?" the pilot asked in conclusion. Everyone shook their heads. The brief was concluded and we assumed the role of the ready crew.

I had already completed a full pre-flight inspection on the aircraft and staged all of my flight gear, so I headed to the avionics shop to use a computer and check my email. Senior Chief had sent me another email reminding me to fill out my dream sheet, which served as a stark reminder that it was nearly time for me to transfer duty stations. With a dream sheet, I got to list which Air Stations I wanted to relocate to in order of preference. The thought of leaving Detroit put a knot in my stomach. I knew it was only a matter of time before I was scheduled to transfer, but it was not a reality I was quite ready to face.

I was raised in Detroit. When I graduated from technical training, I had the option of going to several different air stations, but I chose to return home after so many years away. It was not a particularly coveted air station, so there were some jokes made when I chose it over sunnier and more desirable locations, like Miami or Savannah. A lot of people couldn't wrap their heads around why I chose it. The answer was simple. My dad was sick.

My childhood was filled with lots of laughter, love, and the typical sibling rivalry with my older sister, Sara. She was very much opposite of me in many ways. I'm sure we fought most of the time because I borrowed her clothes without asking or tried to be that annoying tag-along little sister when her friends were around. As years went on, we got closer. My dad getting sick played a big role in that. What I lacked in caregiving skills, she made up. Sara and my mom took care of my dying father day in and day out. While I was away in the military she took the brunt of that. And for that I will forever be grateful. She was, and still is, the real MVP.

"The Leppert Squad," circa 1989:
Mom (Lana), my sister (Sara), Dad (Jim), and me.

My father, Jim (Daddio, my buddy, Jim Shoe), worked extremely hard at the local newspaper press ensuring our family always ate well and had money for all the essential Trapper Keepers and K-Swiss shoes any young teen could need. My love for this man cannot be formulated into words. He was and forever will be my best friend (sorry Mandi Pants). What I can say is that he was so very opposite of me yet my twin in every way. He was a man of very few words. His 6'2" stature and deep blue eyes were coupled with the coolest handlebar mustache ever. His detailed description of his last meal was his favorite conversation to have. I suppose we weren't that different after all. There was a mystery about him that even I, as his daughter had a hard time uncovering. I knew his childhood was a troubled one, riddled with abuse from his father. But my father, the oldest of his siblings, would stand firm and face his drunken father who would beat him daily. My father would tell his younger brothers to hide while he would take the beatings from his whiskey-dazed father. And his eyes told me a story that words weren't needed to express. Those baby blue eyes were often shielded by his favorite Detroit Lions hat. The other half of his wardrobe consisted of his *Macomb Daily Newspaper* uniform that he wore with pride. He was a hardworking man although his lifestyle since his youth was a fast one, filled with sex, drugs, and rock n' roll.

He was hands-down my idol. One of my favorite memories of him was watching the Thanksgiving football game together, with T.V. trays instead of at the dinner table with the rest of the family. He taught me how to play sports and lose with dignity, and better yet, to work even harder to win. I was his shadow. Daddy's girl.

My mom, Lana, was kind and loving. Like my father, she had a troubled childhood. Her bravery was in a class of its own. Her youth was robbed by a family member who molested her before she even reached her fourth birthday. "Nap times" with her ill-minded grandfather snatched her innocence like a thief in the darkness. Her bravery was spotlighted by her ability to protect her younger siblings from having to be exposed by such trauma. She was her sisters' protectors while simultaneously planting a deep wound that would carry into her adulthood and crave the numbness that only alcohol would provide.

I am the full-blooded product of bravery. My parents unknowingly taught me the greatest lesson of my life. It wasn't how to tie my shoes or to say *please* and *thank you*. Rather, it was to be a fearless and brave protector of those who couldn't protect themselves.

Mom took pride in making sure we were dressed in the most stylish 90s neon jumpsuits and windbreakers. She would wake us up early for school so she could tease our wild hair to perfection. We weren't rich, but we had each other. She always put us first and showed me what it was like to be a strong woman. And she called me her "rock." From a child's perspective, life was good. We were happy.

Every aspect of our life was very normal for the average middle-class family. But as the years went on, I began to notice that my family had demons lurking behind the curtain of normalcy. From around the age of 10, I started putting odd pieces together. I would soon be able to see the whole puzzle of addiction quite vividly. The noise of a beer cracking, then turning into a whole case became an every-night routine for my mom. As strong as she was, she was also facing demons from her past. I can't imagine growing up as a young child and being molested and then during your teenage years being with a man who abused you daily. For my mom, those memories dissipated with every drink she had. This addiction only amplified when my father got sick.

> Dear Daddy,
> I MISS YOU!!!!!!
> You know what, I really don't care what the doctor rules are. I am coming in to see you.

My note to my father when he was in the hospital

Trips to the hospital to visit my dad became normal for me at a very young age. He had so many illnesses. When I was in the sixth grade, he had his first heart attack and had to get a quadruple bypass surgery. I was traumatized by the thought of losing my best friend. Hospital visits became routine. So did my anger at the nurses who wouldn't allow me to see him at times. In one letter to my father when I was 11 I wrote: "Daddy I miss you. I don't care if those nurses say I can't come in to see you, I am going to anyways. If they try to stop me I sneak in when they aren't looking. I can't stand being away from you. Squeeze my teddy bear with a hug if you start to miss me."

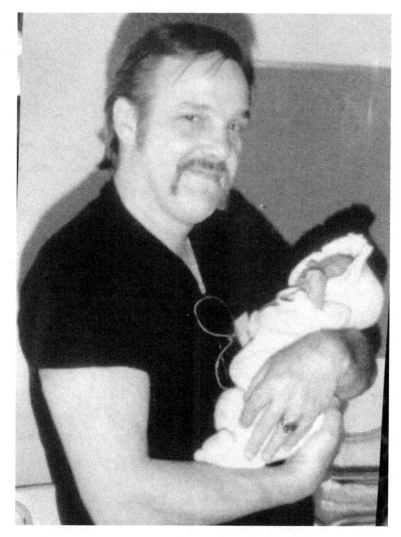

My dad holding me the day I was born.
Check out that sweet handlebar mustache.

The quadruple bypass surgery healed his heart but induced an uncontrollable and ultimately fatal addiction to prescription pain pills. For years this went on. It was only when I got to high school did I realize just how bad it really was. Many terrible memories remain of finding my father's gallon-size zip lock bag full of painkillers or finding him with pools of blood from where he had scratched himself raw from the side effects, or even losing the ability to control his bowels. This created a rage inside of me. I hated those pills and what they did to my father. I would scream and cry, "Dad why are you doing this to us! We love you and can't stand watching you slowly kill yourself." The sad truth was, he wanted to quit as much as we wanted him too. That is addiction. I still have trouble reliving those memories.

Over the years, his health declined even further. He was soon suffering from diabetes, emphysema, and a devastating addiction to pain killers (possibly more drugs that he didn't allow us to find out about). It was so hard watching my dad suffer and worse watching my mother's alcohol addiction only increase. By the time I graduated from technical training in 2009, I knew I had to get home and spend the little time I had left with my father.

I returned home to help my family. My sister and mother were the real MVPs. I couldn't bear to bathe my father, or help him to the bathroom, so I would leave the house and find reclusion in the park or the creek behind the house. I watched my dad slip further and further away, but I cherished every moment I spent with him. In early June of 2010 my father was put on hospice. His organs were slowly shutting down, primarily his heart. I was in avionics technical training eager to graduate but knowing my father wasn't doing well.

I received a call one day from my mother saying I needed to get home as soon as possible because my father wasn't going to make it through the night. After explaining the situation to my instructors, I hopped in my car and hit the road. I was driving about 20 mph over the speed limit with Red Bull and No Doz (caffeine tablets) supplying my adrenaline. I repeatedly prayed to God to allow me to say goodbye to my dad before his passing. This ten-hour drive felt like an eternity. I can still hear the song, "Airplanes" by B.O.B. playing on the radio, on what seemed like every damn station. I still hate that song because it only reminds me of the tear-soaked t-shirt I wore that drive.

I made it just in time to sit alongside my father's deathbed and tell him I loved him so much, that it was okay to leave and meet Jesus and his mother in heaven, that I loved him more than anything on this planet and regardless of his own struggles that he was the most amazing father I could ever want. His morphine-induced coma rendered him speechless but I knew he heard me. He died only a few short hours later from heart failure. I knew he waited for his baby girl to come home.

When he died, I was only 25 years old. I had to be the rock that my mom and sister needed. My mom was so devastated by the loss that she could barely function. Soon after, her dependency on alcohol skyrocketed. Some days she would drink over case of beer herself. She would put on her headphones, listen to classic rock (my dad's favorite), and ride around mowing the lawn for hours on end. She seemed almost at peace when she had nothing to concern herself with except the operation of that lawn mower and a cold beer in her hand.

During this time I turned into this stoic, emotionless figure. I concerned myself with the administrative details. I had to make sure my mother would have enough money to support herself. I helped make the arrangements for my dad's funeral. I had to ensure that my family had all of the things they would need in the wake of such a traumatic loss. Throughout the whole process, I handled the things that needed attention with my shoulders back and my head held high.

I prepared a speech for my father's funeral. In their grief, my mother and sister were unable to deliver an address of their own, so I was faced with giving my father his final farewell. When it was time for me to speak, I walked up to the podium briskly. I looked out into the crowd of loved ones that had gathered to say goodbye to the most important man in my life. I looked down at my speech. I looked back up. Their faces had become blurred as my eyes began to swell with tears. I looked back down at my speech. A few of my tears dripped off the tip of my nose and made the words on that paper, the words that I had chosen so carefully, start to bleed and run. I looked back up at the crowd and found my mom's face.

"I can't do it!" my voice broke. I collapsed over the podium. I pressed my face to that speech and sobbed. Right there, in front of the whole congregation. I didn't care who saw, it felt good to let it out. I cradled my head with arms. Every bit of anger, grief, fear, and despair that I had tucked away over the last few days surged out of me in an overwhelming flood of emotion. I found my mother among the blur of faces. Seeing her gave me the boost of strength I needed to get through these next few moments. With a few deep breaths and a glance back at my father's casket, I composed myself and delivered the speech. I closed with this poem:

> God saw you were getting tired
> And a cure was not to be.

So He put out His arms around you
And whispered, "Come to me."
With tearful eyes we watched you,
And saw you pass away
Although we loved you dearly,
We could not make you stay
A golden heart stopped beating,
Hardworking hands at rest
God broke our hearts to prove to us,
He only takes the best.

    I don't think anything unites a family quite like the pain of grieving, and the loss of my father brought me back together with my mom and my sister. I weaved my way back into familiar routines with a family that I had been physically absent from for years due to my military service.

    But that familiarity was short-lived. Before I knew it, it was time, once again, to be the child that calls often but can only visit seldom. Addiction and an unhealthy lifestyle took my father. As for my mom, she is a survivor of the disease. In 2013, after a nearly fatal trip to the emergency room, that all changed. She suffered internal complications from her alcohol abuse. She told me she laid in that hospital bed and prayed to Jesus to heal her and she would never drink again. Well, the Lord delivered.

    All of those same arguments I had with my father, yelling the typical, "Why are you doing this? Stop this addiction, your family loves you," rang a familiar tune with my mother. I eventually gave up. I was exhausted—physically, mentally, and emotionally. After years and years watching both of my parents battle their addictions I finally came to a realization. I had to worry about myself. Addiction knows no boundaries or borders. I could no longer shave years off of my life by trying to change their behavior. I had control over myself and that was it.

After my mother's sobriety I had a newfound and very different relationship with her. No longer was I on edge around her. My walls crumbled to the floor as I was finally feeling closer than ever with her. She was renewed and so was our relationship.

She has been sober since 2013.

[5] Off the Ground

"Rescue the weak and needy; Deliver them out of the hand of the wicked."

—Psalm 82:4

As I stared at Senior Chief's email, I thought about which air stations I might be interested in. There was only a handful of Coast Guard Air Stations scattered across the United States and Puerto Rico, so that helped narrow it down.

"Do the detailer's even look at these?" I muttered under my breath.

My shoulders and upper back started to tingle a bit. As of late, this sensation had become a good indication that I'm fatigued and should take a break. I started to experience fatigue far more often—so often that it felt commonplace. *Why do I feel this way?* I kept stewing over this in my thoughts. *I guess it's just stress*. It wasn't that late in the evening, but I decided to head to the flight mechanic duty room to rack out (or "hit the sack," as they say).

I got to the flight mechanic room, flung off my boots, let my hair down, and threw myself onto the bed. Sleep embraced me almost immediately.

WOOP, WOOP, WOOP!

The SAR (search and rescue) alarm screamed out of the speaker just outside my door and woke me with a startle. I instinctually jumped up and threw my boots right back on.

WOOP, WOOP, WOOP!

I glanced over at the clock. It was just past midnight.

"NOW, GET THE READY HELO ON THE LINE, GET THE READY HELO ON THE LINE. WE HAVE A REPORT OF AN EMERGENCY LOCATOR BEACON ACTIVATED IN THE MIDDLE OF LAKE MICHIGAN. NOW GET THE READY HELO ON THE LINE . . ."

WOOP, WOOP, WOOP. The loudspeaker repeated the message about the report of a red flare. (A red flare is used as an emergency locating device for people if they find themselves in trouble both in the water and on land. Sometimes this is accidentally used for fun by people not realizing it may be seen as a distress signal.)

I ran into the hangar. The hangar doors were already open and the duty line crew team was towing the ready helicopter outside and onto the line. I ducked into the women's locker room and threw on my thermals, my bright orange dry suit and my vest. My vest contained emergency egress equipment such as a seatbelt cutter and a small tank of compressed air that can be used to escape a water-filled cabin in the event of a crash over water.

I ran out to the helicopter and got there at the same time as my copilot. I strapped on my flight helmet and plugged it into the long spiral cord that allows me to communicate with the other members of my crew on the internal communications system.

"On ICS," I stated.

"Loud and clear," the copilot responded. He was already in the copilot seat and turned on the electrical system.

"I have you the same," I responded.

"Starting number two engine."

The number two engine was on the right side of the aircraft. I stood outside, just next to the pilot's door, while holding up two fingers. I heard the familiar *tick, tick, tick* of the engine igniters just before the engine started to make a high-pitched whining noise. The noise grew more and more intense until it turned into the familiar roar of a jet engine. I made a circular motion with my hand, holding up two fingers to indicate that the engine started successfully. Slowly, the main rotor blades overhead began to turn. *Whoosh.* One blade went by over my head. *Whoosh.* Another one passed. Butterflies fluttered in my stomach as the blades began to pass over my head faster and faster, until I could no longer see the individual blades and a shadowy rotor disk whipped the air around me.

"Engine number two start successful. Starting engine number one."

I walked around the front of the helicopter and stood next to the copilots' door. I held my pointer finger up. With one engine running and the rotor blades spinning, it was more difficult to hear the next engine start, but I could feel the added power. I moved my hand in a circular motion to indicate a successful start and walked back to the right side of the aircraft.

The helicopter's hoist was on the right side of the aircraft. It was essentially a winch that hangs just next to the right-side cabin door, allowing me to lower and raise a hoist hook between the helicopter and the surface below. The hoist was my responsibility. I began my preflight checks as I listened to the copilot go through his preflight checklist out loud. I opened the hatch that was just above my head and adjacent to the cabin sliding door, which allowed me to stand as I operated the hoist. I boomed the hoist in towards the helicopter and back out. I lowered the cable a few feet.

Here I am practice hoisting with a boat crew, 2014

The pilot and the swimmer jogged up to the aircraft with their thumbs raised, seeking permission from the copilot to enter under the rotor arc. The pilot had been getting last-second weather data and information from sector, who dictated our operations. The swimmer needed a bit of extra time with the gear that was necessary for him to perform his specialized role. With a flash of the aircraft's taxi lights, indicating that it was safe for them to go under the rotor arch, they approached the helicopter. The pilot hopped into the pilot seat. The swimmer, with his fins and goggles in tow, double checked the operation and security of the hoist hook I had just lowered. He jumped into the aircraft and strapped into the swimmer seat that was on the floor in the back of the cabin. I utilized the hydraulic cut off to make sure my hoist would still operate in emergency mode and then I closed the hatch and the sliding door. I jumped into the flight mechanic seat, which sat just behind the two pilot seats, and I strapped on the five-point harness. I swiveled my seat around to take a look at the swimmer. He gave me a thumbs up.

"Ready aft," I said.

The pilot was on the radio with air traffic control, clearing us for departure. "Coming up," she announced as she gently pulled up on the collective flight control with her left hand. The helicopter made a distinct increase in noise as the collective changed the pitch of the rotor blades, creating enough lift to raise the helicopter off of the ground. We came into a hover. The pilot, copilot, and I kept an eye on the instruments in the cockpit to make sure everything was operating properly and that we wouldn't exceed any limitations. The pilot nosed the aircraft down by pushing the cyclic forward. She simultaneously pulled up on the collective, increasing power and bringing the helicopter into forward flight.

Only minutes had passed between the first wail of the SAR alarm and the time we got airborne. Initial takeoff was always accompanied with heavy radio traffic as the pilots talked to tower, sector, and other aircraft. The swimmer and I stayed quiet and kept our eyes outside to spot obstacles or traffic as the pilots worked their way through their task-saturated phase of flight. The pilot broke her silence once we cleared heavy traffic and were en route to our search location. "Okay. We've had a report of a red flare. Sector has given us the search pattern. We'll arrive on scene and fly the pattern until we've located a survivor or until we're called off."

Red flare—no matter what the call was for, we would always hustle to get on scene and start responding to an emergency or searching for survivors. But I had to admit that my heart sunk a little when the SAR alarm was followed with the words "red flare."

There's a feeling that every child gets when they receive a birthday card in the mail. There's a spark of excitement that ignites when they get their hands on the card and see that it's from someone with a history of spoiling them, like a grandparent or an aunt. As they rip the card open, they are already imagining what they'll do with the money that they are so certain lies inside. And then they open the card. No money falls out. There must have been a mistake, so the child double checks the envelope. It too is empty. The child's heart sinks as she or he realizes that the only thing enclosed in the card is a handwritten birthday message from the sender. That was what it felt like to go flying on a red flare.

"Has anyone ever responded to a red flare and actually rescued someone?" the swimmer asked.

"Not that I know of," responded the pilot.

"Can't say it's happened to me," replied the copilot.

"Hmmm, nope, not me either," I contributed to the conversation. "I know someone that flew on a white flare sighting."

"I've never heard of a white flare," said Mr. Tritchler.

"Is that even a thing?" asked Nate.

"Don't think so," I said. "And apparently there was some big meteor shower that night, so that crew was pretty certain sector sent them out to investigate a meteor sighting."

Nate laughed. "Ha-ha! Just like how we always get launched for flare sightings on July 4th and New Year's. I've flown on more firework sightings then I care to remember."

The conversations stopped and nobody spoke on ICS for a while. The helicopter was quiet aside from the roar of the engines and the beating of the rotor blades. We reached our search pattern starting point and began flying a series of parallel lines over the water. The full body vibrations caused by the helicopter was soothing. While I concentrated as hard as I could on scanning the water for signs of distress or anything unusual, I prayed: "God, if someone is in trouble, give me the eyes to find them."

The vibrations of the helicopter alone can cause shaky vision, and I was also wearing night vision goggles, or NVGs, which are even more disorienting. They are particularly disorienting when scanning the water, because water has no discerning features, like buildings or trees. I slipped my fingers behind my NVGs and rubbed my eyes. I looked back at Nate in time to watch him stretch his arms and let out a large yawn as he looked out the window and scanned the water.

0045. The helicopter continued chugging along and flying in straight lines, turning occasionally to fly in the other direction. We didn't spot anything at all, let alone anything unusual.

"We should play the alphabet game with aircraft parts," suggested the copilot.

"What in the world is that?" I asked.

"We name an aircraft part that starts with A and then work our way through the alphabet."

Not a bad idea, I thought to myself. It might keep us engaged and help us stay up.

There were a bunch of methods we came up with to deal with long flights in a search pattern. The method was usually dictated by the composition of the crew. At times a crew would stick to more wholesome conversations about places to travel and eat. Some crews would swap stories about their various rescues. Others would spend the flight helping each other study emergency procedures or aircraft systems. A particularly rowdy crew would swap hilarious stories. These stories were usually told by rescue swimmers and almost always had something to do with women they were seeing. Occasionally I would crack the crews up with my dating stories, as I have quite the laundry list of hilariously terrible first dates. Often times our stories were too inappropriate to repeat, but they would make us laugh 'til our stomachs hurt. They passed the time and kept us alert, and that was all that we needed.

"I'll start," said the copilot. "Accelerometer."

"Blow down bottle," said the swimmer.

"Compass, magnetic," I said.

"Can she do that?" asked swimmer, almost offended.

"Why not?" said the pilot, sounding like an uninterested substitute teacher refereeing an argument between two kids. "Directional Gyro."

I swiveled my chair around to face the swimmer, threw up my arms and mouthed, "What are you going to do?" He flipped me off facetiously.

"ELT," said the copilot.

"First limit indicator," I chimed in.

The game continued on for three whole repetitions of the alphabet. I'm sure we repeated a few components, but none of us seemed to notice or even care. The game kept us engaged as we continued to fly the search pattern and looked out over the water.

0200. I called sector on the radio and let them know that we were thirty minutes to bingo, or thirty minutes until we need to land because of fuel depletion. A few minutes later, sector told us to stand down from SAR and return home.

"Yay," said Nate, mid-yawn.

0230. The helicopter made its way back to Air Facility Muskegon and landed. The duty line crew came out to fuel the aircraft and perform the thru flight so the pilots, swimmer and I could head back to bed quicker.

The pilot kept the debrief quick. "Good work," she said. "Let's get some rest."

"I think we should revisit the alphabet game rules," said Nate. "It's a magnetic compass, not 'compass, magnetic'."

"Bro, you're a rescue swimmer, do you even know what that does?" I joked and pushed his shoulder.

"Go to bed guys," Lt Donaldson said. She laughed and walked away to call the operations boss and give them an update. After turning to Nate and flashing a gloating smile, I headed to the flight mechanic room. I got to the room, threw off my boots, let my hair down and threw myself onto the bed. Sleep embraced me almost immediately.

WOOP, WOOP, WOOP!

The SAR alarm screamed out of the speaker just outside my door and woke me with a start. I instinctually jumped up and started throwing my boots on.

WOOP, WOOP, WOOP!

I glanced over at the clock. 0300. Less than 15 minutes of sleep.

"NOW, GET THE READY HELO ON THE LINE, GET THE READY HELO ON THE LINE. WE HAVE A REPORT OF A KAYAKER IN DISTRESS…"

Like a robot, I begin to tow the aircraft back out the hanger, pre-flight the helicopter, and wait for the aircrew to join me for take-off. After a detailed ground brief, we learned that the kayaker had activated his emergency locator beacon. The coordinates showed he was in the middle of Lake Michigan. I crushed some cold coffee I found in the hanger maintenance control room and we were enroute. After a quick aircraft start we head to the passed coordinates.

Not after 20 minutes of flying the sun began to peak over the horizon. As a crew, you can sense the adrenaline rush of focus. This wasn't a red flare, but rather someone we knew for certain was in desperate need for our help. After a very thorough rescue brief, I call out "MARK-MARK-MARK," which is an indication for the pilots to mark the position because a survivor has been located. "Two o'clock, 100 feet." As we closed in, I made out the silhouette of a kayaker waving his paddle and retching violently, clearly dehydrated and in bad shape. We rapidly began rescue check two, which occurs when we are in a hover and begin to lower the rescue swimmer and rescue device. Within minutes he was safely in the helicopter and we were headed back to the air facility where an ambulance was waiting.

The man we rescued was trying to kayak from one side of Lake Michigan to the other. Thankfully, he was prepared enough to have the personal locating beacon so if things did get bad, he had an out.

"Always have an out." Those words echo in my head from an old executive officer I worked for. They couldn't be truer.

The day closed with us logging one life saved, making the local news and even a video on YouTube. But something else happened that day. I was renewed. Every long maintenance hour I spent fixing discrepancies, every long sleepless duty night, every birthday spent on duty, every Christmas spent away from family, every single sacrifice I had made up to that point was all worth booming this guy into the helicopter cabin and seeing his eyes look into my soul saying, "Thank you." This is what I lived for, and it would set the stage for a bigger scene that I could have never imagined, right at my new unit, Air Station New Orleans.

[6] NEW ORLEANS

"The most effective way to do it, is to do it."

—Amelia Earhart

I BRUSHED A stray hair away from my face as I blankly stared at the computer screen in front of me. I was supposed to be filling out the maintenance logs for the aircraft I was just working on, but fatigue set in and I took a minute to myself. The New Orleans heat brought a whole other element to my confusing health issues. It's really easy to chalk up fatigue and muscle weakness to the extreme levels of heat and humidity. Eventually, I decided to snap back to it. As I completed my work, I looked at the box that auto-fills the time and date.

Man, I thought to myself. *I've already been in New Orleans for six months.* Air Station New Orleans wasn't too much different than Air Station Detroit. After all, operating procedures were standardized throughout the service and it was the same type of people bouncing from one air station to the next. It was the environment outside of the Coast Guard that changed drastically for me.

The move from Detroit to New Orleans was difficult. You don't have to visit either city to know that they are vastly different in culture and character. I'm a very adaptable person, so I thought that the change in scenery would be pretty easy, but it proved to be more challenging than I anticipated.

In Detroit, I got used to being around my family and friends again. Even after years away from home, I fell right back into the comfort of being able to drive just a few miles to meet a childhood friend for brunch, or play on my longtime softball team, or run into an old high school teacher at the grocery store. I had been able to extend my tour in Detroit and spent five-and-a-half amazing years there before being told it was finally time to transfer. Sometimes I thought of my tour in Detroit as bittersweet. It was such a blessing to be close to family but having the ability to serve in the Coast Guard while being close to home made it so much more difficult to pack up and ship out when the time came.

In New Orleans, I was acutely aware of each birthday I missed, each family activity I couldn't participate in, and each holiday I had to miss out on. I could no longer take part in the smaller nuances of everyday family life. I had to jam-pack as much bonding as possible into the rare opportunities that I had to visit a few days at a time.

Anyone that has to leave home for work will tell you that the best thing to do is to immerse yourself in your new location. Find clubs to join, social events to go to and explore the local culture and cuisine. No matter where you are, there is something awesome to be discovered about that place.

In Detroit, I was the source of strength for my family and friends. In New Orleans, it would soon become apparent that I would be the one needing help. Certain life events that I had tried to ignore were slowly surfacing in the solitude of my new environment.

ONE OF THE ACTIVITIES I dove into in New Orleans was CrossFit. I discovered the Marrero CrossFit gym shortly after arriving. Starting with the intention of working on my physical fitness, which was becoming more and more difficult to do, I also found an incredible support network. I was also able to exercise my spiritualism in a wonderful new church called Vintage New Orleans, introduced to me by coworker Colton Courtway.

"You can leave when you finish your paperwork," my chief said as he walked by me in civilian clothes, clearly on his way home himself.

"Thanks, chief. See you tomorrow!"

As soon as I finished my paperwork, I logged off the computer, grabbed my stuff and started walking to my car.

"Ashlee!" It was Maegan Miller from across the parking lot. "Do you want to dinner and wine?" Maegan Miller and I had quickly grown to become best friends. She was my shoulder to lean on during some of these tough transitional months. She was a beautiful and intelligent flight mechanic. I was proud to work alongside her.

"It's Tuesday!" I yelled back. "I've got CrossFit, but maybe after." I threw my stuff in the backseat of my car, grabbed my phone and looked up the workout I could expect once I got to the gym. "This one is going to kick my ass," I muttered to myself. "Good."

I rolled the windows down, turned some music on and started driving. It was a hot, sticky day in New Orleans, but I still felt the need to have some wind blowing through my hair instead of blasting the air conditioning. "No love" by Eminem came on my Pandora shuffle and immediately I was dancing in my seat on my way to the gym. "Yes!" I yelled to myself as I reached over to turn the music up. I started singing. I waved one of my arms around and emphasized the notes I was hitting. I was bouncing around in my seat. At a traffic light, I glanced over and noticed that a man on the side of the street was looking at me with a half-smile and raised eyebrows. I gestured to him, leaned out the window a bit and started singing even louder. He chuckled nervously but maintained a look that could only be described as a combination of confusion, amusement, a tinge of fear and *This woman is crazy!* I didn't care. I spread the love. Make people smile and laugh. *I felt good.*

I pulled up to the Marrero CrossFit gym to meet my best buddies Danielle and Dylan Hernandez. They were the first ones to introduce me to the gym, after much resistance. In true CrossFit fashion, the gym looked like it used to be some type of storage facility that was retrofitted to accommodate a gym. I didn't need fancy buildings or state-of-the art luxury amenities to get a good workout! I parked my car, grabbed my water and walked into the gym.

I felt a sense of calm wash over me as I looked around at all the weights, rowing machines and pullup bars. This gym became a bit of refuge to me after the move from Detroit.

I did my rounds throughout the gym, saying hi to everyone and engaging in the regular small talk that occurs before beginning the workout of the day. Most people gave me a half-awkward smile, probably wondering to themselves how this new girl could walk right in and act like she was at home. But I did. Every day. As the instructor announced that it was about time to start the workout, I paired up with Anna and Nate Laviolette. We started with push-presses and push-jerks. I was on fire! I was tossing around the weight and felt unstoppable. My partners were complimenting me and cheering me on. I burst into a huge smile and kept pushing. When it was their turn, I was cheering them on.

After push-jerks, I got on the floor and into a plank. I tucked my elbows back and went down until my chest nearly touched the floor and then I pushed back up. *One*, I said to myself in my head. Again, I went down and up, performing a solid pushup. *Two*, I said in my head. Something didn't feel right, so I decided to pause for just a second while holding a plank. Suddenly, my elbows buckled and the floor rushed towards my face. My arms simply gave out!

"Ashlee!" I heard Anna scream.

Wow, what had just happened?

My arms just stopped working. What the heck?

I tried to push myself up into a kneeling position but failed to find the strength. Instead, I rolled over onto my side and pressed a hand firmly on my face and over my nose to help soothe the throbbing pain. This was terribly embarrassing.

What is happening with my body? I thought to myself. I'd been battling this internally for months now.

"Ashlee, are you okay?" Anna asked as she put a hand on my shoulder.

"Yeah," I muttered as I pulled my hand away from my face to check for blood. No blood. Good.

"Can you stand?" Coach Rustin asked.

"Yes, just give me a second," I responded, clearly embarrassed and frustrated.

I started pushing on the ground to roll myself into a seated position. My partner helped me out. I appreciated her assistance, but I couldn't help but feel a tinge of annoyance. I sat on the floor for another minute or so with my elbows resting on my bent knees and my face buried in my hands.

"What happened?" Coach Jonathon inquired.

"I have no idea!" Anna exclaimed. The tone in her voice clearly expressed her confusion. "She was doing pushups and then she just fell and hit her face."

"How does someone just fall and hit their face?" asked another man in the gym that had gathered to witness the commotion. Here we go, I thought. They all must think I am faking it. *No, something is wrong*, I thought. I put my hand up with my forefinger slightly extended to stop their conversation. They became silent. Eventually, I peeled my face away from my hands and looked up. It seemed like half the gym stopped what they were doing to come and stare at me. I felt the sudden need to get the hell out of there.

"Alright," I announced quietly as I propped one of my arms behind me and attempted to stand. My partner helped me again and I made it to my feet.

"Are you woozy?" Coach Missy asked.

"No, I'm fine." To an extent I was telling the truth. I didn't feel unsteady. "I'm going to get out of here."

"Are you okay to drive?" Coach Nick asked.

My skin felt like it was starting to crawl. Too many people were looking at me and asking questions. I grabbed my water bottle and bee-lined it towards the exit.

"Yes, I'll be fine. I'll text one of you when I get home safely," I yelled over my shoulder.

I briskly walked to my car and threw my water bottle into the back seat without looking back. I jumped in, started the car and backed out of my parking spot. I waved to them to indicate that I was fine and they waved back. They didn't go back in. They stood there, continuing to watch me with a look of concern until I was out of view. I stared at the road in front of me, wide-eyed and slack-jawed.

"What the hell just happened to me?" I asked myself as tears began welling up in my eyes. I ran the last few minutes at the gym through my head, looking for some explanation. I felt fine during the push-jerks. I didn't feel light-headed and the room wasn't spinning. I drank plenty of water all morning. I felt normal when I started to do the pushups, and I never had trouble with pushups before. My arms just gave out after two. The loss of strength in my arms happened so suddenly that I didn't even have time to prevent slamming my face into the floor from a plank position.

The Hurricane Within

"Two pushups," I said to myself out loud. "That's what you can do now."

My hands started trembling as I struggled to fight back the inevitable flood of frustration. I scrunched my face and blinked rapidly to fight back the tears that were welling up in my eyes. I found myself driving home in a trancelike state, just kind of on autopilot. I don't actually recall the drive home, I just know I got there.

I jolted back to reality when I hit one of the pot holes that New Orleans is so famous for. I was on my street. It was an older neighborhood with brick sidewalks, plenty of trees and brightly painted houses that were decorated with various purple, yellow, and green ornaments, protected by wrought iron fences. I parked my car on the street, put on some sunglasses and started walking to my door.

As I was walking I saw my landlords, Karen and Vince, who became a part of my New Orleans family, and who I affectionately called, "Oma and Paw." They were out on their front porch and enjoying some wine, in what we called "porch duty." I tried to flash them a big smile and wave, but the best I could muster up was some type of grimace. My brain would tell my muscles what to do, but my muscles seemed to develop selective hearing.

"Oh man! That wine looks good!" I said to them. "I might be doing the same thing soon after the day I've had!" I forced a joke as I passed by.

"Come on up and join us!" Oma said back.

"I might take you up on that! I've got a few things to handle first but I'll let you know."

She smiled and Paw raised his glass to me before taking a sip, "We just cracked a bottle and its porch duty time."

I tried to conjure a smile as I walked under their carport to the front door of my apartment. My apartment used to be their basement before they refinished it to be a one-bedroom, fully equipped apartment. I loved my little home.

As I grabbed the keys to unlock my door, I could feel that I had exhausted every bit of energy that I had left. I was physically unable to face anyone else that day. I opened the door, and there stood my beautiful black lab, Mandi, wagging her tail, looking up at me with her big black eyes, lifting her legs up and down, performing those tippy taps that dogs do when they are excited. My heart exploded. Every bit of emotion I had been forcing back poured out of me. I leaned back on the door and slid down until I was on the ground and eye level with this precious animal. She instantly recognized my mood. She crawled into my lap, which she was entirely too big for, and started to lick at the tears that had begun to run uncontrollably down my face. I wrapped my arms around her and squeezed her tight.

We stayed there for what felt like hours. My shaking and sobbing eventually receded to stillness and small sniffles. I was praying for answers and clinging to the unshakable faith that Jesus provided me. Mandi stayed still, leaning against me. Occasionally she moved to nuzzle her head into my neck. Every so often I heard the lethargic *thud, thud, thud* of her tail wagging and hitting the floor. I just kept wondering what was wrong with me. That was on a replay reel in my mind.

It dawned on me that she needed to go out and hadn't been walked since I left for work in the morning. I squeezed her just a bit tighter and buried my face in her fur. She was so selfless.

She was probably dying to go for a walk, but decided it was more important to stay still and provide comfort in a way that only a dog can. I lifted my head up. "You want to go for a walk Mandi girl?" I said it in that baby voice that is also appropriately used on dogs. She jumped up, resumed her tippy taps and started wagging her tail. I pushed myself up, grabbed her leash which was attached to a bright pink collar, and readied her for the walk. I took a quick glimpse of myself in the mirror and decided to throw my sunglasses back on.

We went out the front door. My landlords had gone back inside. The streets were fairly quiet, just the usual light foot traffic of other dogs walkers and locals enjoying a stroll towards their favorite café or bar. Mandi trotted in front of me, making sure she didn't miss any curious smells along the way.

A few blocks into the walk, I felt my phone vibrate. My mom was calling.

"Hey Mom," I answered.

"Hey sweetie. I was just thinking of you and wanted to see how you're doing," she said.

"Well that's just sweet of you!" I exclaimed. "Is that my niece I hear playing in the background? How's she doing? And how are you holding up Mom?"

"Oh she's good. She discovered she really enjoys playing in the dirt lately and has been busy doing that. I'm fine. I've been up to the normal things. Your sister has been busy taking the girls to karate, dance—any activity she can sign them up for, she's such a good mommy!"

"Well that's good to hear. I'm always worried about you guys. I miss you!" As I said this, I deeply wished we could be having this conversation in person.

"Are you doing okay baby girl? Your voice sounds really hoarse."

"Yeah, I'm fine," I said very unconvincingly. "I'm just under a lot of stress and I think it's starting to affect me physically."

"Is it work?" she asked.

"I'm not sure. Work hasn't been particularly stressful. I just feel like I need a break from everything."

"That doesn't sound like the Ashlee I know. Do you remember playing roller hockey when you were a kid?"

"I loved roller hockey."

"We knew from the start that we were going to have our hands full with you," she laughed. I cracked a smile and managed a small chuckle. "You were always playing in the mud and getting dirty. And you played every sport under the sun; baseball, soccer, basketball. There was no keeping you in the house."

I continued listening to my mother as I walked with Mandi. I stopped to sit down at a bench that overlooked the levee and the city of New Orleans.

"Well, one day you decided you wanted to play roller hockey with all of the neighborhood boys," she continued. "You begged us for a pair of roller blades for months. You asked us for a pair of roller blades so often that your begging became a bit of an inside joke between your dad and I."

The Hurricane Within

"I couldn't have been that bad!" I joked.

"Oh yes you were," she shot back. "Anyways, we broke down and bought you a pair for Christmas. Your face lit up when you opened that present and you were so excited."

"I remember opening that present like it was yesterday. And the hockey stick!"

"Well, it was winter in Detroit, so you obviously couldn't wear them right away. We thought you were obsessive when you just wanted the roller blades, but you became worse when you had them but couldn't use them!" she joked.

"That's like torture for a kid!" I laughed.

"As soon as summer came, you strapped those things on and rode down to the end of the street. You were so excited."

"I bet you were excited to have some quiet in the house after that winter!"

"Children are a blessing," was all she said in response to my joke. "Well, you were only gone for about fifteen minutes. You stormed through the front door and went straight to your room. I went to check on you and you weren't crying, but you were very upset."

I stopped with Mandi and looked over the water. I pet Mandi on the head as I recalled the story my mom was telling. I remembered the pain of being rejected and being told I couldn't play roller hockey because I wasn't a boy. I could vividly recall how hurt and confused I was. I was good at sports and had already beaten most of those boys in other activities. Why should roller hockey be any different?

"My heart broke for you," she said. "You insisted on being left alone, so I left you in your room, but I spent the rest of the afternoon thinking of other things you could spend your summer doing instead of roller hockey."

I started laughing. "You should have known better!"

"I should have! The next morning, you strapped those roller blades back on and went down to the end of the street. Just like the day before, you came back in about fifteen minutes and stormed straight to your room."

I stood up after giving Mandi one last scratch behind the ear and started walking along the levy and back towards my house.

"Three weeks, Ashlee. You went down to the end of the street and got told you couldn't play every day for three weeks. I was beginning to get really worried about you. And then one day, I forget what I was doing, but it hit me that you didn't come home. It was getting late and I was starting to wonder where you were. Just as the street lights came on, you stumbled into the house. Your knees were bloody, you had ripped a hole in your shirt, your arms were covered in bruises and on your face were streaks of dirt, and a giant smile."

"That was a fun day," I said with a small smile on my face. "They finally said I could play."

"And you didn't just play roller hockey every day for the rest of the summer," my mom said, "those same boys that said you couldn't play started ringing our doorbell to invite you to out."

"Being stubborn pays off."

"It does," she started laughing. "You've always been stubborn and pushed through. Keep your head up."

"Thanks Mom," I said quietly, trying to keep my voice from cracking.

I could hear some commotion in the background on my mom's side of the phone. My niece was squealing happily and I could hear my sister yelling her hellos throughout the house. "Your sister just got home. I have to go, but we'll talk soon, okay?"

"Ok, Mom. I love you."

"I love you too."

I hung up just as I was approaching my house. I was still tired, and had no desire to socialize with anyone, but I felt much better than I did just moments earlier. My mom was right about one thing, I was stubborn. More importantly, I had never been afraid to walk straight up to something and face it head on.

Mandi and I walked inside. I opened my phone and sent myself a reminder to make an appointment with the flight doctor in the morning.

Ashlee

Ashlee is so special! She can make you laugh when you are feeling really down, or if your day has not gone right. She can be so funny with her imitations of people. She lights up my life. She makes me happy. She can make a gloomy day turn into a bright sunny day. She protects her parents, meaning no-one better say mean things about her parents, or people that she loves or cares about, because that person will have to pay! ROYALLY!!!!!

Ashlee is very much into sports and loves to play many of them, but I'd say her favorite is soccer. She told me that when she goes to Junior High, she wants to sign up and become a player! Well I tried to explain that to her, that there are no girls on the football teams!!!!!! She did not like hearing that. She feels things should be more equal!

Ashlee at twelve is so tall, so pretty. She has such a good shape, and loves to exercise with out even knowing she is doing the exercise. She rides her bike a lot and stays very active. She does many things to keep her busy.

Ashlee has a great imagination. She can invent things and also come up with ideas about certain things, or if she is playing with her friends, she will come up with some really neat things to do.

This is gonna be a hard year for me. Ashlee will be going into Junior High School next year, and leaving Elementary School after being in that school for eight years. She is excited about leaving elementary school, which I can't blame her, but as her mom it is very

A letter my mom wrote about me, 1997

[7] THE SPECIALISTS

"That is why we never give up. Though our bodies are dying, our spirits are being renewed every day."

—2 Corinthians 4:16

"**HEY ASHLEE**, how are you? What's going on?" the flight surgeon asked me, cheerfully. The flight surgeon was responsible for ensuring we were fit to fly and, like a primary caregiver, was the first point of contact for any medical concerns.

"I'm still having problems. I still feel very weak sometimes."

"Let's see." He said and started scanning through my medical records. "Last time we spoke was for your annual flight physical and you said that sometimes you found it difficult to chew your food and your facial muscles felt really weak at times."

As I sat there listening to the flight surgeon scroll through medical records, I began to reminisce about all the crazy things I'd seen and done throughout my last 12 or so years in the Coast Guard. On my very first trip on an aviation detachment crew we helped seize cocaine from a Caribbean smuggler. That was followed by rescuing a boat of six Cubans who were adrift at sea, then detaining a *yola* (a small boat) with over 100 Haitians on board, representing the Coast Guard for the 2012 major league baseball playoffs and picking the game ball on the field, and even meeting President Obama while on a temporary duty trip as part of a rotary wing air intercept team. The memories kept coming. *The things I had seen and done up until this point,* I reminisced, *and now my muscles can barely smile, I can barely do a push up, and I even have trouble chewing my food at times!*

"That's one of the things that's bothering me," I explained. "Sometimes I can't smile. I try to, but I can't. And lately I've caught myself slurring my words."

"And you think these symptoms are getting worse?" He asked, sounding concerned.

"Kind of, some days I feel great and others I've been feeling really weak. Twice this month I struggled to pull my shirt off before jumping in the shower and then yesterday I collapsed and fell on my face when I tried to do a pushup."

"Is it possible you were just fatigued? You work out nearly every day, you have a very stressful job. You work long hours and they can be random and chaotic. And you are in your thirties now."

"That's what I thought at first," I said. "I know my work takes a lot out of me and that I would have to deal with getting older, but I'm not so sure that's what this is anymore. I've been feeling different for several years now and I have been doing everything I can to combat it. I've changed my diet, forced myself to go to bed earlier, I've reduced alcohol intake, and I workout more. I've also started taking dietary supplements to help me feel more like myself, like magnesium. But I haven't felt any improvement in my overall wellbeing. If anything, I feel like I'm getting worse. I'm gaining weight, I'm not improving my physical fitness despite the fact that I'm spending more time in the gym and eating better and I just feel so tired."

The flight surgeon maintained eye contact with me throughout my entire explanation and I appreciated his attention. When I finished, he looked back down at my medical records and continued to thumb through it.

"I know this isn't what you want to hear, but I think we need to focus on the issues you're having with your jaw. The things that concern me are your difficulty chewing and the issues with smiling and speaking. Since you joined the Coast Guard, you've had a clearly documented case of temporomandibular joint syndrome. As you know, this causes pain and popping in your jaw. Normally, it's not that serious of an issue but perhaps we need to look into it more."

"I've had popping in my jaw for years and it's never really bothered me," I said.

"Perhaps it's a symptom of a deeper problem. I think we should start there. I'm not dismissing the other symptoms, but I think it's more likely that they're the natural consequence of an active life and natural aging. Keep up the healthy diet and sleep."

He swiveled his chair to the side to face a computer screen and then started typing away on the keyboard. "I am going to refer you to a dental specialist for his opinion. Do you think it's affecting your ability to do your job or fly?" he asked.

"No sir, I am good to fly and stand duty. Hopefully, it's just my jaw causing me problems."

He finished typing and grabbed a sticky note next to his keyboard. He scribbled on the note and then handed it to me. "Sounds good. You can go there now."

I looked down at the sticky note that contained the dentist's information. "Thank you, sir."

"We're just taking it from here, okay? We'll keep talking after you hear from the dentist," he said with a sympathetic tone. He could sense my disappointment.

I nodded my head. "Yes, sir. Thank you so much for your time"

I stood up, wished him a good day and headed out. My head was swimming as I recalled all of the symptoms that I didn't think could be explained away with jaw problems. I got to my car and grabbed my phone. I opened Google and typed in all of the symptoms I'd noticed in the last few years.

Blurry vision, trouble chewing, can't smile, muscle fatigue, tired…

The Google results listed a number of terrifying diseases: multiple sclerosis, chronic fatigue syndrome, myasthenia gravis, mitochondrial disease—My heart skipped a beat as I started to skim the list of horrifying possibilities. I clicked on one of the diseases to read about its properties, symptoms, and treatment options. Then I clicked on another disease, and then another, and then another...

I found myself going down the "what if" rabbit hole. I started finding the possible correlations between every disease I was reading about and the symptoms I was experiencing in my own life. Some of the diseases seemed like a perfect match, so I went to several different medical websites to learn all that I could about them. Sometimes only one or two of my symptoms would be listed under a particular disease, but that didn't stop me from learning everything I could about that disease as well. I would start with one article, then click on a hyperlink that led me to a suggested article, then click on another hyperlink. At some point, I start imagining what my future might look like if I were indeed suffering from the disease I was reading about. Would I be able to take care of myself? How would I work? Who would pay for the treatments?

A truck that was parked next to me started suddenly, jolting me out of the Google hypnosis. I looked up at the clock on the dashboard and realized that I had been sitting in the car and staring at my phone for 45 minutes.

"Crap," I said to myself. "This is why you don't self-diagnose."

I threw the phone onto the passenger seat and started driving.

I WAS SITTING in the dentist's office. After Googling myself into an oblivion, I decided to leave my phone in my pocket. I looked around the small room to find something that I could read to entertain myself. The walls were decorated with the standard medical facility posters. There was a chart with six or seven different cartoon faces displaying happy, healthy teeth on one end, and a scrunched-up face displaying excruciating tooth pain on the other end. There were other posters advertising smoking cessation seminars, grief counseling, food planning courses and other health related educational courses. On one of the cupboards, someone had taped up a "sound alike medication" cheat sheet that listed a number of drugs that people often got mixed up. I wasn't quite sure how I felt about that.

I soon ran out of things on the wall to read, so I stared at the floor in silence. After a significant period of waiting, I heard a gentle tap on the door and the dentist came in. He was a soft-spoken man with a gentle and focused demeanor.

"How are you today?" he asked.

"Oh, I'm doing fine," I drew out my words just a bit as I spoke.

"So, you are here because of the issues you have been having with your jaw?" he asked as he thumbed through my record.

"That's part of it. I've been having trouble with fatigue, sometimes my vision stays blurry and, I don't know, sometimes I feel like my muscles just give out. But the doctor says he wants to focus on the problems I'm having with my jaw, so he sent me here."

"You've had popping in your jaw for years, I see."

"Yes."

"I'm going to put my hands on your face and just feel your jaw," he started washing his hands in a small sink in the corner of the room. He walked over to where I was sitting and placed his fingers just below my ears on the jaw. "Open and close your mouth."

I did as he asked and, as expected, my jaw made the small popping noises I had become accustomed to.

"Well, it's definitely popping," he said. "This is not something I deal with regularly. I'm going to refer you to a maxillofacial surgeon."

"A what?"

"Maxillofacial surgeon. They are the guys that focus on treating the hard and soft tissue of the face, mouth and jaws. If a more invasive procedure needs to be performed to correct jaw alignment, for example, then they are the ones to talk to."

I sat there silently and looked at him. I knew he had just told me some information about the next medical professional I would go see, but all I heard was *I don't know what's going on so I'm going to hand you off to someone else.*

"Do you have any questions?" the dentist asked.

"No."

"Ok. Go to the front desk, they'll set up your appointment and hopefully the specialist can give you some better answers."

"Thank you, sir."

"Take care," he said as walked out of the room.

I got up and walked down the passageway to the front desk. The woman there wrote down the information for my next appointment, which I learned was in two weeks. With a "get it done" personality, two weeks was a long time to wait.

That evening, I sat down with a cup of coffee and started working on my game plan. I found an article that discussed how acupuncture could be used to relieve muscle tension and release the jaw for free movement, so I booked an appointment with an acupuncturist. I found another article that praised the effectiveness of going to a chiropractor for muscle fatigue and jaw problems, so I booked an appointment with a chiropractor. I found a physical therapist in my neighborhood that focused on helping people with muscle fatigue and booked a consultation with her as well. I found an article about massage therapists and their ability to relieve the pain related to temporomandibular joint syndrome. I booked an appointment with a massage therapist. Admittedly, I was more interested in treating myself to a massage at this point and the article gave me a good reason to do so.

I looked up from my phone, yawned and threw my arms back into a giant stretch. I felt the knots in my back crunching as I squeezed my shoulder blades together. Everything around me was a bit blurry. I had spent far too many hours on the phone for one day.

THE VARIOUS APPOINTMENTS I had set up to explore my symptoms via other alternatives were a healthy distraction. However, they were all a swing and a miss as far as viable treatments are concerned. The acupuncturist couldn't answer any of my questions and kept leaving the room to ask her colleagues for advice. This left me with little confidence in her ability to do her job. After she left the room for the fourth time, I saw myself out. The chiropractor spent a lot of time working the muscles in my jaw, which did feel nice, but then she started talking about how frequently I should return for the most optimal results. She said that I should stop in at least once a week to see any significant improvement. I politely told her that I'm not made of money. I found the physical therapist to be the most frustrating. Before I even got a chance to discuss my concerns and tell her what I was hoping to gain, she started talking about her pricing and the various packages I could buy. The consultation didn't last long. The massage was heavenly. We didn't even discuss my symptoms. I just treated myself to a much-deserved break.

The day arrived for my appointment with the maxillofacial surgeon. A small fountain in the corner of the room made peaceful bubbling noises and every so often the sing-song voice of the pretty blonde lady behind the gray marble reception desk called the name of a patient. The floors were dark wood laminate, which went nicely with the green, leafy plants scattered throughout the space, and the seats were nicely cushioned and upholstered with faux leather. It felt more like the reception area for a spa then a medical facility.

"Ashlee?" the receptionist called out in a soft voice.

"That's me," I stood up and start walking towards her.

"Follow me, please." She opened a door next to the reception desk and guided me down a hallway to an empty room. She gestured for me to take a seat, told me that the surgeon would be in shortly and then gently shut the door behind her.

The exam room matched the esthetic of the waiting room. The room, while well-lit, lacked the harsh fluorescent lights that were so often associated with hospitals. The walls were painted a soothing color of teal blue. There was a noticeable absence of medical posters or flyers. The exam chair, the only indication that I was in a medical facility, was eggshell in color and offered a lovely contrast against the blue wall.

I pulled out my phone to occupy myself as I waited for the surgeon. I made the decision to hold onto what little sanity I had left and avoid Googling my symptoms. I browsed through the news, skimmed through my emails, and wrote a few texts to friends I hadn't spoken to in a while.

I heard a firm knock at the door and a man in a lab coat walked in. He was tall with brown hair and chiseled facial features. He reminded me of a Ken doll. He flashed a smile, with teeth that seemed obnoxiously white, and held out his hand for a shake.

"Hi Ashlee, I'm Dr. Johnson. How are you doing?"

"I'm doing well, how are you?"

"I can't complain." He sat on the stool next the chair I was sitting in, leaned forward a bit to place his forearms on his knees, and established eye contact with me. "So, I looked through the notes your dentist sent over and he says you're having problems with your jaw popping. Can you elaborate on that for me?"

"Sure," I said. "I've always had issues with my jaw popping. But lately I've had issues chewing and smiling. I've also been really tired and my muscles seem to just give out on me, but I'm not sure how that ties into my jaw."

"I see. Do you mind if I do a quick examination of your jaw? I'd like to see how your jaw movement feels."

"Of course not," I said as I scooted forward in my chair a bit.

He stood up and placed his hands along the side of my face, with his fingertips resting gently at the back of my jaw and just under my ears. He made small circular motions with his fingertips and slowly increased the pressure. He ceased motion and remained still for a moment.

"Now open your mouth as wide as you can."

Just as I began opening my mouth, I felt my jaw pop and I stopped opening it.

"Keep going if you can," he instructed.

I continued to open my mouth without any issue until it was wide open.

"Now close."

I closed my mouth without any popping or clicking.

"Let's do that again," he said.

I opened mouth and, as before, it popped, but I continued to open it fully without any further issues. I closed it without any problems.

"That's a pretty violent pop you have in your jaw," he said.

"Yes, it's always been like that. It's never really bothered me."

"I'm going to suggest corrective jaw surgery," he said and took his position back on the stool next to me.

"Surgery?" The inflection in my voice betrayed my shock.

"Yes. Basically, we would break your jaw and then reset it. I know that this sounds excessive, perhaps a bit scary, but it's the same concept as someone having any other bone in their body broken and set in place after improper healing."

I watched him as he spoke, but kept my mouth shut. I had no words.

"In performing this procedure, we would be attempting to reposition your jaw into its natural position, which, if successful, would eliminate the popping and any discomfort you have associated with the popping."

My head started to spin. I remained silent while I processed the information he was communicating to me.

"You look a bit perplexed, Ashlee. Perhaps I can answer some of your questions to make you feel more at ease about the whole process."

"Let me get this straight. You want to break my jaw and then reposition it."

"Essentially, yes."

"And if you're successful, then the popping in my jaw would go away."

"That would be the ideal outcome, yes."

"What are the odds of it not being successful?"

"As with all procedures, there is no guarantee of success."

"Ok. Can you give me an idea of the odds of it working?"

"About 50 percent. I know at first glance, that doesn't seem that high, but you need to consider the benefits if it does correct all these problems you're having with your jaw."

"You want to break my jaw for a coin's flip chance that the popping in my jaw, which has never really bothered me, might go away."

"It's a lot to take in. Some of the key phrases involved in the procedure are off-putting, I know. How about you take some time to think about and we'll stay in touch."

"Thank you," Out loud I spoke politely. In my head I began to scream, *What the hell is wrong with this guy?*

He rose from his stool and exited the room swiftly. I sat for a moment in the spa-like room with my brow furrowed and my mouth gaping. Two weeks ago I fell on my face because my arms gave out, and today I was being told that my jaw needed to be broken so I could address the popping. I struggled to understand the correlation between the two. I snapped out of my daze and headed home.

As soon as I found the comfort of my couch, and after giving Mandi some well-deserved attention, I pulled out my phone and typed a reminder to myself to call the flight surgeon for an appointment the following week. I set the phone on a small stand next to the couch. I leaned forward and cradled my face in my palms. I focused on my breathing in attempt to calm my mind. My head was swarming with information, some useless, from all these medical appointments. I dropped my hands and exhaled a long sigh. I looked over at the phone for a few seconds.

I stood up and headed to the kitchen. I grabbed a glass and poured some wine into it. I stood in thought for a few minutes, my back leaning against the fridge and one arm wrapped around my mid-section. I took small sips of the wine and stared at the other side of the room with unfocused eyes.

After a few minutes, I made my way back to the couch, tucked my legs up by my side and covered myself with a blanket. I turned on the TV and absentmindedly chose a cooking show to watch. Text messages kept pinging from my friends at home checking on me, knowing about my whirlwind of appointments. *PING*, Erin McPhail, I ignored it. *PING*, Lindsey Kennedy, I ignored it. *PING*, Caitie Pomorski, I ignored it.

I turned my head back to the TV. A chef was teaching proper techniques for roasting a duck. I wasn't interested. I turned my head to look over at my phone again. I stared at the phone for a bit and then turned my head back to the TV. Now he was chopping up vegetables. This attempt at distraction was useless. I reached my hand out and snatched the phone off of the table. I sat up, crossed my legs and hunched over the screen. I opened up Google. With shaking fingers, I began to type: *Blurry vision, trouble chewing, can't smile, muscle fatigue, tired...*

[8] Something Bigger

"You, Lord, give perfect peace to those who keep their purpose firm and put their trust in you. Trust in the Lord forever; He will always protect us."

—Isaiah 26:3-4

I WOKE TO the familiar tune that meant it was time to start another day. While it was once a cheerful tune, classical conditioning now caused me to despise the noise. I had been meaning to change it for a couple of years. My eyes didn't want to open and it took some effort to do so. I slowly managed to force them open as I sat up in my bed. The world around me was blurry. I didn't expect anything to come into focus for a while as I had stayed up far too late Googling myself into oblivion, once again. I poured some coffee, threw on a flight suit, kissed Ms. Mandi goodbye, and headed out the door to work. Today, I was on the schedule to stand flight mechanic duty. I was looking forward to a lighter workload and the possibility of flying on a search and rescue case despite the feeling of fatigue, like I hadn't slept at all.

I arrived at work and walked across the hangar to chat with a few people before attending the oncoming duty crew brief.

"Look who decided to show up!" joked Kyle McClure from on top of a helicopter that was under heavy maintenance. He looked like he was inspecting the main rotor head. Kyle McClure was one of my oldest friends in the Coast Guard. Stationed together for over eight years we've managed to stay friends longer than most people's marriages. The Coast Guard wouldn't be the same without seeing Kyle every day at work.

"Very funny!" I joked back. "I've had some medical appointments lately."

"Nothing serious, right?" Nic Ferrante popped his head up and asked as he was bent over an engine. Nic Ferrante was one of my last students that I took flying as a flight mechanic instructor. We joked back and forth like brother and sister. Like Nic, I looked at most of my Air Station New Orleans co-workers like family.

"I don't think so," I said. "Just taking precautions."

"Be careful with that," another mechanic said. Leaning over the engine he dropped his tone to a more serious note. "You can get grounded for the craziest stuff. I had a buddy in Miami get grounded for some random allergy they couldn't pinpoint."

"I know," I said. Nobody wanted to get grounded, which meant you were unable to fly until you were cleared by doc to do so. There was a love/hate relationship between aviators and medical. As an aviator, you got the best medical treatment. You didn't have to remember when you needed new immunizations or routine blood work, as you would be reminded by medical when they needed you to come in. You were constantly monitored and any potential health issues were addressed pretty immediately.

On the other hand, any issues with your health might lead a flight surgeon to determine you were no longer fit to fly, or you might get grounded for a while until the cause of some ailment was better understood. As a result, whether it was right or wrong, aviators were very careful about what they shared with medical. An off-handed comment could raise a red flag and start the long, drawn-out process of properly addressing the medical concern.

The basic rule of thumb was to use common sense. If an ailment could be treated or addressed without involving a medical professional, then it was best to keep it to yourself. However, everyone was expected to be an adult and know when their issue was beyond their ability to treat and required medical attention. You didn't find too many hypochondriacs in aviation.

"Hope you're okay!" he said as I kept walking across the hangar.

Out of the corner of my eye, I saw one of my coworkers rushing towards me and waving his hand to get my attention.

"Ashlee!" he shouted and I turned to face him.

I warned, "Please don't tell me I have to be the watch captain tonight because you didn't finish your qualifications." I had been looking forward to standing flight mechanic duty for a while and tonight's schedule was contingent on this man finishing his watch captain syllabus. The watch captain was in charge of the duty crew and worked the logistics behind launching and recovering a helicopter for search and rescue. This person stays behind as the rest of the crew flies off to complete the mission.

"I'm really sorry," he said. My heart sank a bit and I did my best to hide my frustration.

"So I have to stand watch captain and you're taking my flight mechanic?" I asked.

"Yes, that's what I was told."

"You had weeks to get this done," I said but instantly realized that expressing my frustration would get me nowhere.

"I know, it's just that I had . . ." and he listed off a myriad of excuses but I wasn't really paying attention.

"Alright, I've got some work to do before the brief," I said curtly. I turned my back to him and walked off. I knew, *shit happens.*

I spent the next few hours performing the mundane work required of the position I would begrudgingly hold this evening. I talked to the off-going watch captain to see if he had any pertinent information about the last duty day. I briefed the pilots on the status of all the aircraft and let them know they didn't have to worry about flying into a maintenance window on the ready bird. I made sure the airmen standing line crew duty had checked the fuel farms and had prepped the towing equipment.

After completing all of the mandatory work, I found that I wasn't ready to turn in for the day. I walked onto the hangar deck and saw that several mechanics were still working on an inspection.

"You guys need a hand?" I asked.

"We could always use an extra body," a mechanic replied as he put a few tools back into their foam cutouts in the toolbox. "I'm about to do blade pins if you want to pop the blade for me."

"I can do that."

I looked towards the nose of the aircraft and saw that someone had already staged a check stand there. I walked to the rotor blade that was closest to the stand and checked to make sure nobody was near the main rotor head or tail rotor.

"HEAD'S TURNING!" I yelled.

I jumped up, grabbed the blade and began to walk it over towards the stand. All four rotor blades slowly rotated around the head above the helicopter while the tail rotor spun at a much more rapid pace. With the blade running directly over the nose of the aircraft and ending over the check stand, I jumped up on the check stand, put both my hands around the edges of the blade and waited.

The mechanic swiftly climbed up the side of the aircraft and positioned himself on top of the helicopter, just next to other end of the blade that I was holding onto.

"Pop it!" he yelled.

The rotor blades on helicopters hung limp and drooped when they were at rest. I lifted the blade over my head, countering the blades tendency to droop downwards and relieved the tension on the rotor blade pins that held it in place. Using small motions, I shook the blade up and down as the mechanic pulled on one of the two rotor blade pins. The pin began to wiggle out slowly for about an inch and then popped out with such force that the mechanic's hand shot past his face.

"Out!" he yelled.

I stopped shaking the blade and lowered it down. I let it rest on my head and kept both hands firmly on both sides of the blade. With only one pin holding the blade in place, it could now pivot to the left or the right, so it was important to keep it still. As with a lot of helicopter parts, the blade wasn't very heavy so it's easy to handle.

The mechanic wiped the blade down, inspected it for damage and corrosion, and wiped a layer of white lubricant on it. He leaned over the blade and looked into the hole he was about to return the pin to.

"Come up!" he yelled.

I pushed the blade back up over my head and locked my arms out.

"Come to the right just a bit." He could see that the holes were not lined up properly, so I moved the blade slowly to the right. "Stop," he commanded.

He stuck the pin in. He managed to get it in about an inch before it got hung up.

"Pop it!" he yelled.

I began to shake the blade up and down while he applied downward pressure on the pin. The pin slammed down into place with a gentle thud of metal-on-metal contact.

"In!" He turned to look at me. "Ready?"

I nodded my head to indicate that I was ready to pull the second pin. With the blade still held up above my head, I began to shake it as he pulled on the pin. As before, the pin wiggled out slowly for about an inch and then popped out of the blade suddenly.

"Out!" he yelled and he repeated the process of inspecting and lubricating the pin while I waited patiently.

As before, I allowed the blade to drop down and rest on my head while I held onto both sides of the blade.

"Come up!" he commanded when he was ready to put the pin back in.

I pushed up on the blade, but it didn't move.

"Come up!" he repeated.

I tried to push up on the blade again but it didn't move. The mechanic looked up from the holes he was trying to align and looked at me. I was standing there with a blade resting on my head and had a confused look on my face.

"Come up!" he yelled louder.

At this point, another mechanic stopped what he is doing and looked at me. "Do you need me to get that?" he asked.

"Yes," I said.

He quickly ran over and hopped onto the check stand. The mechanic standing on top of the helicopter squatted down and got his head below the blade. He was clearly concerned that if I lost control of the blade, then it might swing around and seriously injure him. I felt the weight of the blade lifting off my head and hands as the other mechanic took control of it. He verbalized that he had positive control and I stepped off of the check stand. The two of them aligned the holes, popped the blade, and got the pin in almost immediately.

The mechanic on top of the helicopter faced me, leaned over the blade and rested part of his upper body on it. "You okay?" he asked.

"I'm fine," I said. "I don't know what happened. I just couldn't push it up."

"I've seen you do this a hundred times, girl. What's the deal?"

"I don't know, but thanks for the hand homie," I responded quietly.

"Make sure you take care of yourself. We've got it from here. You should go to the crew's lounge and chill for the rest of the night."

"You're probably right."

Embarrassed, frustrated, and defeated, I walked out of the hangar and headed to the crew's lounge. I got to the door and could hear the TV was on. I put one hand on the door frame and rested my forehead on the door. Unable to gather the energy to go in and interact with the rest of the duty crew, I turned away and decided to find the watch captain's bed and go to sleep.

WOOP! WOOP! WOOP!

I shot out of bed and instinctually grabbed for my boots.

"NOW, GET THE READY HELO ON THE LINE, GET THE READY HELO ON THE LINE. WE HAVE A REPORT OF A MAN OVERBOARD…"

I got my boots on and began to jog to the hangar while throwing my hair up into a messy bun. The line crew airmen were already opening the hangar doors. Out of the corner of my eye, I could see the duty rescue swimmer sprinting to grab his equipment. I jumped into the tug and, with a thumbs up from the airmen, I began to tow the aircraft out of the hangar and onto the line. I parked the aircraft with the nose into the wind and before I had a chance to get out, one of the airmen disconnected the tow bar from the aircraft for me. As I was driving the tug and tow bar back into the hangar, the copilot hopped in and began his preflight checklist.

Within minutes, the flight mechanic and rescue swimmer arrived at the helicopter. I heard the *click click click* of the engines starting to fire up and the rotor blades beginning to turn. The pilot in command finished gathering last-minute information about the case and local weather and ran out to join his crew. The noise of the rotor blades increased suddenly and the aircraft slowly peeled itself away from the ground below. It came to a hover about fifteen feet off the ground, dipped its nose down, and flew off into the night.

I turned to the airmen. "Good work guys," I said. "You got over here really quickly."

"We were still up playing Call of Duty," one of the airmen replied as he reached for his energy drink.

"Man that looks good! I wish I could have one!" I said enviously as I pointed at his drink. He smirked and shrugged his shoulders. Aviators on flying status were not allowed to consume energy drinks. "Well, you guys can get out of here. There's no point in you hanging around here. Just listen for the pipe about the crew returning."

As they turned and walked away, they immediately resumed their conversation about video game strategies. I began to meander around the hangar, finding small things that were out of place and returning them to their proper homes. I was never good at going back to sleep with a crew out on a case.

In all likelihood, they would be gone for a couple of hours. Despite my best efforts, feelings of jealousy began to creep in my mind. For a brief moment, I found myself hoping they would only fly a boring search pattern. After all, I was supposed to be standing flight mechanic duty, and the man that took my position only did so because he didn't get qualified in time. *Let it go*, I thought to myself. I loved the guy, he was a good friend so I didn't mind taking one for the team.

I decided to settle into a comfortable office chair in the maintenance control office and watched some mindless TV show.

SEVERAL EPISODES of a mindless sitcom helped pass the time before I heard the familiar announcement over the loudspeaker that the ready aircraft was inbound and estimated to land in ten minutes. I stretched my arms overhead, threw my head back and yawned audibly before walking back out onto the hangar. The two airmen made their way onto the hangar with their heads hunched over and leaned in towards each other. One of them was making very dramatic gestures with his hands as his mouth moved quickly with excited chatter. They must have been playing a very exciting game.

The helicopter landed near the hangar and shut down. The moon was glistening in the stark backdrop of the sky. The humidity was still extreme, even this late at night. The airmen and I walked towards the helicopter and waited for the rotor blades to come to a complete stop before going under the rotor arc. While the airmen started pulling out the fuel hose and hooking it up, I went to the sliding door on the side of the helicopter where the rescue swimmer and flight mechanic were getting out.

"Any issues?" I asked, as addressing any maintenance concerns on the ready bird were my top priority as the watch captain.

The flight mechanic turned around and the swimmer popped his head out the door. They were positively beaming. I instantly recognized the look of a post-rescue high.

"No maintenance problems," the flight mechanic replied.

"But a good flight though?" I asked.

"It was crazy!" the rescue swimmer jumped out of the helicopter excitedly and went into story telling mode. "This dude on a shrimp boat got stabbed! They threw him overboard and then, I don't know what their deal was, but then they decided to call for help. We found him and I jumped in. He was bleeding all over the place and I was like, *please, no sharks!* But we picked him up and got him to a hospital. He'll be okay. His friends are probably screwed though! Pretty sure the cops will have something to say about it." His voice began to trail off. "I'll be back. I've got to clean this blood up."

I looked into the cabin and there was indeed a decent amount of blood pooled on the floor and smeared against the avionics rack panel. I heard the fuel pump kick on and turned around to face it. The flight mechanic was holding the dead man stick—a hose that controls the flow of fuel from the pump to the aircraft.

"You don't have to help turn the plane around!" I said as I started walking towards him. "Go get some sleep, in case you get called out again."

"I don't mind," he said.

"Sounds like you had an exciting case!"

"Yeah, it was pretty cool." His level of his excitement didn't quite match that of the rescue swimmer.

"What's up? Why aren't you more pumped? This is what we stand duty for!"

"It was supposed to be your case, Ashlee."

I paused for a second. He was right. After my initial struggle with jealousy, I was surprised I didn't feel a resurgence of that emotion upon learning about the rescue.

"I'm happy for you. We all did our job tonight and someone is alive because of it."

He nodded in agreement and looked at me with a half-smile.

"I'm proud of you guys." I smiled back.

"Come on, give me that thing," I said as I grabbed for the dead man stick. "Seriously, go get some sleep."

"Thanks, Ashlee."

He walked away and I helped finish refueling the aircraft.

I felt an incredible calmness course through my veins and throughout my body. By all accounts, I had every reason to be bitter. However, I had no need to fight any feelings of jealousy or bitterness because the feelings simply didn't exist. I had always heard stories of people hearing the voice of God. It was a concept I never understood because I had never experienced it. Deep down, I always thought it was just something people said. But standing still and looking at the bright orange helicopter in front of me, I felt a euphoric sensation in my chest. It was a feeling that can only be described as a mix between the warmth that is felt when you are embraced by someone you love and the excitement you feel when something you have been dreaming about comes true. This feeling began to make its way to the rest of my body as it crept down my legs and arms and all the way to my fingertips and toes.

I didn't hear anything, but I *felt* a message that I knew was coming from God. He said, "Be still my child, I have something way bigger planed for you."

[9] The Beach

"No, I never saw an angel, but it is irrelevant whether I saw one or not. I feel their presence around me."

—Paulo Coelho

EVERY NOW AND then, I would go out of my way to get selected for training that got me away from the air station. It was always a good opportunity to take a breather, meet some new people, and expand my knowledge base. I found myself in Pensacola attending Applied Suicide Intervention Skills Training. I decided to take full advantage of the entire trip. I took in as much information as possible during training, as it was a topic that struck close to home. At the end of the training day, I took the time to turn my focus inward and work on my own mental well-being.

THE HURRICANE WITHIN

After my father passed away, my mother told me she had thoughts of suicide. The idea of living life without her husband was a thought too harsh to bare. She admitted to me that once, after an alcohol fueled bender, she went into the garage, turned on the vehicle, and sat as the invisible carbon monoxide filled the air. It was in that moment of almost ending it all that my sister and I flashed into her mind. She rediscovered her will to live and she quickly turned off the vehicle. This saddened me to my core when I found out. This suicide intervention training was very near and dear to my heart.

"Meeting the Angel" beach day, Pensacola August 21, 2017

At the end of the training day I went back to my hotel room and changed into my swimsuit. I packed a bag with some water, a towel, and a book, and then headed to the beach. The beach was walking distance from my hotel and I took my time getting there. As I walked, I made a conscious effort to acknowledge the good in my life. I appreciated the opportunity to receive valuable training, I appreciated the beautiful weather, and I appreciated my body's ability to enjoy a casual stroll.

Thank you, God.

The beach was surprisingly empty. There were a few people here and there but it was, for the most part, empty. I found a nice spot on the beach that was close to the water but in no danger of getting wet and threw my towel down. I pulled out my book and began to read. I had started a book called *When God Winks at You*. So far, the message I'd received from the book was that God was always with us, even when our life seems uncertain and overwhelming. He communicated this to us through little miracles.

The book was hitting very close to home. Between the stress of moving away from family, not understanding what was going on with my body, and my failure to get any answers from medical professionals, I was beginning to feel powerless. I was beginning to feel like I was losing control of my body, my mind, and my life. When I needed it most, I felt the presence of God and it filled me with a sense of reassurance and calmness.

I looked up from my book and took in the beauty of the water and the beach. I closed my eyes for a bit and said a quick prayer to thank God for the ability to experience such things. I opened my eyes again, put my book away and grabbed a water. I looked around the beach and saw an older man about a hundred feet away, sauntering in my direction. He was wearing a dark, loose hanging shirt and jeans that had been cut off just below the knee. He looked like he was wearing a backpack and he was carrying a couple plastic bags that appeared to be filled with clothes or small blankets. As he got closer I could see that his dark skin looked worn and excessively wrinkled from too much time spent in the sun. His clothes were stained and hung heavily from all of the sediment collected.

He caught my curious gaze and started to walk directly towards me. I felt a twinge of panic—I had no intention of interacting with this man. My mind raced as I tried to decide if I was going to get up and leave or stand my ground and ask him to leave me alone. He stopped about five feet short of me. I was still sitting and I looked up at him uncomfortably. He fixed his gaze on the ocean in front of us, set his plastic bags on the ground and sat down. He put the soles of his feet on the ground, leaned forward, placed his crossed arms on top of his elevated knees and continued to watch the ocean.

We sat in silence for a minute. As time passed, the man began to feel less like a threat and more like a curious stranger. He didn't seem to want anything from me. He pulled a pack of gum out of his pocket and took a piece for himself. He then extended the hand holding the pack towards me to offer me a piece.

"No, thank you," I said.

He continued to look at the ocean.

"I'm going through a hard time," he said suddenly. "I keep questioning God. I know I shouldn't, but I do. I don't know what to feel."

I was taken aback. I hadn't come to the beach expecting to engage in conversation with anyone. And I definitely didn't expect to be approached with a conversation that paralleled my own struggles.

I told him, "I really believe that God always comes through," and he turned to look at me. In stark contrast to the rest of his appearance, his dark eyes were sharp, alert and focused. "Sometimes I feel alone but then He always finds a way to reach out and remind me that I am not." The conversation deepened a bit and I reassured him that through the promises of the Bible, we need not fear, with verses like:

> "Do not worry about your life, what you will eat; or about your body, what you will wear. Life is more than food, and the body more than clothes. Consider the ravens: They do not sow or reap, they have no storeroom or barn, yet God feeds them. And how much more valuable you are than birds! Who of you by worrying can add a single hour to his life? Since you cannot do this very little thing, why do you worry about the rest?"
>
> —Luke 12:22-26

The wrinkles at the corners of his eyes intensified as he smiled and gently nodded his head. He turned his gaze back toward the water.

"I appreciate your words," he said with a smile of approval.

After a moment, he stood up. He collected his belongings slowly and deliberately. He turned to look at me and his sharp eyes made contact with mine.

"God bless you," he said, "You are going to change people's lives."

With a smile and a sense of empowerment he turned to walk away. I watched as he resumed his slow saunter down the beach. I got head-to-toe chills as I watched him saunter down the beach. I turned away for one last scan of the beautiful Pensacola Beach waters before I left as well. When I looked back in his direction, he was nowhere to be seen.

Ready to fly!

Part Two:
Hurricane

[10] Briefing

"Do nothing from selfish ambition or conceit, but in humility, count others more significant than yourselves."

—Philippians 2:3

JUST A FEW days after returning from Pensacola Suicide prevention training, I was on backup duty for the 27th of August 2017. Back up duty means that if the primary duty flight crew for the day gets "bagged out" in flight hours (flying for the maximum allowed six consecutive hours), then the backup crew is called in. I had heard some whispers of hurricanes brewing in the Gulf of Mexico, but at this point all the projections showed was that the hurricane was headed far west or might even dissipate before hitting landfall. I prayed to God to protect everyone in the path of the storm, unaware that my crews and I would be playing a pivotal role in rescuing over 50 men, women, and children.

0400. I was woken up suddenly by the ringing of my phone. I usually left my phone on silent throughout the night, so the ringing was particularly disturbing. Disoriented and groggy, I reached for it.

"Hello?"

"Hey Ashlee, I'm sorry to wake you, but are you ready to head out to Houston?" The calm and gentle voice of my engineering officer, LCDR Larry Santos was coming through the phone. I abruptly sat up in bed and the events of the previous evening came flooding back into memory. Hurricane Harvey had made landfall, and I was put on call to respond. As was the case with most hurricanes, the extent of damage was unknown, so Coast Guard crews from all over the nation were put on call. Most of the time, the news media would exaggerate the severity of the storm so I wasn't expecting to get a call.

"Yes, sir," my voice was suddenly alert as it hit me that I was receiving the call every Coastie hopes to get.

"Get to the air station as soon as you can. We're leaving as soon as the whole crew gets here."

"Yes, sir. I'll see you soon."

LCDR Larry Santos was a soft-spoken and laid-back powerhouse. As the engineering officer of the air station his skill level was unmatched. He had the respect of the entire hanger deck for his fair yet firm way of doing business. I felt safe flying with him.

We hung up and I jumped out of bed. I threw on my flight suit and boots. I grabbed my flight bag which was pre-staged and contained a couple sets of undergarments and a spit kit. I called and texted my dear friends Dylan and Danielle, who had previously agreed to watch Mandi Girl if I got called out and told them I was headed into the air station and the key was under the front door mat. After a quick trip to the bathroom I brushed my teeth and wrangled my hair into a semi-neat bun. I kissed Mandi Pants goodbye, grabbed my small packed bag, and headed out of the door within minutes.

I had the most relaxing yet adrenaline-filled drive into work that morning. With the streets unusually quiet, my racing heart was almost audible. Realizing I was driving in silence, which was a rarity for me, I turned on my radio to my usual station, KLOVE. The most calming and fitting song was playing, "Eye of the Storm," by Ryan Stevenson. I was acutely aware of the real danger I was about to face, yet I felt a sense of calm run over me. I smiled and thanked God for that reminder. I had nothing to fear with the Lord by my side.

I arrived at Air Station New Orleans and found it unusually lively. The on-duty line crew airmen had already pulled out the helicopter destined to respond to Harvey. AST2 Bob Hovey, the rescue swimmer who was put on call with me, was going over his equipment in the helicopter. I walked over, threw my small bag into the baggage compartment and jumped into the cabin to help.

I was happy when I found out Bob was going out as my rescue swimmer. We had flown together so many times that the ease of hoisting with him was almost palpable. He always matched my sense of humor and political views, which made a lot to chat about on those long duty nights. I respected him and valued his work ethic both in the Coast Guard and his fishing charter business. The rapport we had built proved to be instrumental in the hours to come.

An airmen popped his head into the cabin and said, "The pilots are ready to brief."

Bob and I headed to the briefing room and sat down with the pilot and copilot. The pilot and copilot were already sitting at the conference table, looking over paperwork.

As he looked up from his paperwork LT Andrew Breen said to us, "Good Morning. Glad to see everyone is here. "We're going to leave as soon as we can, but not before we have a thorough brief. We are flying into a hurricane. I don't think I need to spell out how serious that is, so let's start going over our contingency plans for weather."

LT Breen and I had many flight hours together as well. We also did a few temporary duty trips together, staging our aircraft in other locations for search and rescue during busy holiday times. He was an amazingly skilled pilot who could keep the steadiest hover in the worst of conditions. In that moment, looking around at my crew I realized, I couldn't have selected a better group of gentleman to fly with. *My crew*

LCDR Santos pulled up a map on the screen behind him. A large, red box sat over the Houston area, indicating that the Federal Aviation Administration had placed a TFR (temporary flight restriction) over the area. Only search and rescue aircraft were permitted within the airspace. "Visibility is going to be far below our training minimums," he said. "We're going to have our heads down in the cockpit, scanning our instruments, often. Ashlee, back us up. Keep scanning the airspace and say something if we hit clouds, or if you see both of us with our heads up. We also need you to be our third set of eyes in the cockpit. Make sure we maintain proper attitude and altitude."

I nodded. He turned his head and began speaking to Bob.

"Since you can't see anything in the cockpit from where you sit, keep your eyes outside and scan for traffic and hazards." He stood up to point at the map. "We can't make it there in one bag of gas. We'll have to refuel. Since the weather is so severe and erratic, we need several contingency plans."

He began to discuss different options for refueling. He pointed out and discussed about a dozen different of them, each one carefully selected based on a possible weather or diversion scenario. This level of planning may seem redundant to some, but it could easily save our lives if we found ourselves flying blind and running low on fuel.

"Finally," he said as he turned his back to the map and sat back down, "we're about to do urban search and rescue. Most of our training is in open water with boats. We're about to hover and hoist next to trees, telephone poles and wires. I cannot stress how important it is to remain vigilant and report all of our obstacles. Does anyone have any questions?"

LT Breen, Bob, and I gently shook our heads and in unison responded, "No, sir."

"Alright, let's go."

Without another word, we stood up and walked to the aircraft together, snapped a quick picture, and off we went.

We were airborne and heading towards Houston by 0600.

My first crew, from left to right, AST2 Bob Hovey, me, LCDR Santos, LT Breen, prior to departing New Orleans en route to Houston.

[11] RESCUE

"The Category 4 hurricane had a diameter of 280 miles with winds of 130 mph during its first landfall. It was downgraded to a tropical storm and made another landfall near the Louisiana-Texas border. Harvey has now busted the US record for rainfall from a single storm, dumping 51 inches of rain in parts of Texas. The coastal cities of Beaumont and Port Arthur got 26 inches of rain in 24 hours. By Sunday, it had dumped 27 trillion gallons of rain over Texas . . . Two estimates put total losses at as much as $75 billion."

—https://www.cnn.com/specials/us/hurricane-harvey

I SAT IN the flight mechanic seat, just behind the pilot and copilot as we continued our flight to Houston. The weather was getting steadily worse and worse. Light showers turned into heavy rain and visibility was reduced to near zero. We were getting close to Houston.

"We should refuel in Beaumont," the LT Breen's voice came over ICS, the aircraft's internal communications system.

"I agree," the LCDR Santos said.

The pilots identified the pre-briefed refuel point in Beaumont and start to descend. I could hear the wind howling over the roar of the engines and the turning rotor blades. The rain was so heavy that we couldn't see anything in front or below us. I turned my head to the cockpit and monitored the instruments. The RADALT indicated we were 500 feet, 400 feet, 300 feet, 200 feet, 100 feet. Finally, the ground below us started to come into view and the helicopter came to a hover. The wind was gusting violently, pushing the aircraft all over the place, but the pilot remained calm and set the aircraft down surprisingly softly.

"Nice," the copilot commented.

The pilots began to look around the airfield we just landed in. We could barely make out the fueling locations. The pilot gently pushed forward on the cyclic (like a control stick on an airplane) and started taxiing the aircraft. The copilot leaned forward and jerked his head, clearly looking for something.

"There should be a taxiway coming up on the right," the LT Breen said.

The rain was so heavy that we could barely see ten feet in front of us. We continued to taxi, very slowly. As we were coming up on it, the taxiway came into view on the right. We took the turn and continued creeping forward. Just in front of us, a faint shadow started coming into focus.

"I think that's the fuel truck," the LT Breen pointed to the shadow.

"Yeah, I think that's it," the LCDR Santos agreed.

The pilot eased back on the cyclic, and the helicopter came to an even slower taxi as the gray shadow started to come into sharper focus. We parked next to the fuel truck and the pilot shut the aircraft down. He turned around to face me.

LCDR Santos instructed, "Alright Ashlee, you're up. Nobody's here, but we've been told the keys are in the truck. We're fueling ourselves. But first we need to find a safe place to park. If the rain doesn't let up at all we will have to put this baby in a hanger until it's safe to fly out. For now, we need to taxi over to this building and see if there is a spot to bring her in. We need you to hop out and check this building to see if it's safe."

"Yes, sir." I took my flight helmet off and unbuckled.

I went to open the cabin door. As soon as I twisted the handle down, the howling wind began to whistle loudly as it tried to fight its way into the aircraft. I tried to push the door open, but the wind was working against me. I threw my shoulder into the door to push it out and then slide it backwards. Rain started pouring into the cabin and splashing up into the cockpit, so I jumped out quickly and closed the door behind me.

I tucked my face down and used a hand to shield my eyes from the pouring rain. I ran towards the open hanger to investigate its condition. I glanced up at the ceiling and there was a gaping hole that water was pouring through. The torn metal roof was thrashing in the wind and looked as though it was going to cave any minute. I ran out to the helicopter, already soaked to my core, and relayed what I had seen.

The Hurricane Within

"Guys, it's bad in there. No safe place for us to hanger. The roof is pretty much caving in and rain water is spewing through. I suggest we refuel quickly and get the heck outta here before it gets worse. And it will get worse," I said. We agreed as a crew to try and make it safely out of there.

As we were told, the keys were in the truck, resting in the cup holder. I grabbed the keys and started the vehicle. I looked over to see that Bob, my rescue swimmer had also jumped out. He grabbed the fuel hose from the truck and ran it to the aircraft. He hooked it up to the helicopter and I found the dead man stick to start the fuel flow. He ran back over to me.

"They want 120 gallons," he yelled directly into my ear. Even so, I could barely hear him.

I gave him the thumbs up, squeezed the dead man stick and started fueling. He continued to stand next to me.

"You can hang out in the truck," I yelled at him.

He shrugged his shoulders, raised his eyebrows and held his hands out to catch some of the falling rain. He was making a point. We were both drenched, it was useless to try and stay dry. We finished fueling, put everything away and hopped back into the helicopter.

"Alright guys," LCDR Santos said after we closed the cabin door. "We've just heard from the air station in Houston. They are completely swamped. I reviewed the weather and there's a window to take off—Let's brief and roll!"

Within 10 minutes we were airborne. Although we were soaked and shivering, you could feel the adrenaline buzz silently bouncing through the helicopter as we headed to save some lives. Once in Houston's airspace, Ellington Field, Air Station

Houston came into view and we landed to quickly drop off our bags. LCDR Santos gathered us around to relay our mission that he had received from Air Station Houston's operations center. The emergency calls were endless.

"Okay guys let's brief. We've gotten a report of a heart attack victim in a flooded neighborhood not far from here. Let's give our aircraft a good thru-flight inspection and get airborne safe and quick," he stated with a calm yet urgent tone.

We finished the brief and headed out to helicopter.

Zero visibility at Air Station Houston (you can barely make out the wind sock at the other end of the ramp) August 28, 2017

MY SENSES BECAME hyper-alert as we flew towards a reported heart attack victim. It's difficult to explain the type of excitement I felt when I embarked on a legitimate-sounding search and rescue case. I wasn't happy, because that would infer that I was glad about someone else's misfortunes. I was simply engaged and laser focused on the task at hand. It was an exhilarating sensation.

LT Breen questioned the crew: "I see the subdivision. He's in the house at the end of the cul-de-sac. It looks like we have enough room to hover the cul-de-sac and drop the swimmer. What do you think?"

LCDR Santos answered: "It looks like a perfect spot to lower Bob. Let's just be careful about the power lines. They'll be in front of us with our nose into the wind. Let's hover relatively high so we can fly out if we lose an engine."

As they discussed the plan, I put eyes on all of the landmarks they were discussing and made a mental note of them while simultaneously going through my rescue checklist and preparing the cabin for a hoist. I was surprised LT Breen could see the power lines right away. These are the reasons I was grateful to have such a solid and seasoned crew. The rain was so heavy that everything around us was dark and gray. I couldn't see the power lines until we were nearing a hover.

The aircraft came to a high hover.

"Opening the cabin door," I announced to the pilots.

I twisted the cabin door handle, pushed the door out and then slid it back. I was hit with a sheet of rain and blasts of wind. Water instantly started pooling on the cabin deck and the wind created little ripples on top of the puddles. With effort, I pushed my body into the wind, opened the hoist hatch and came to a standing position. I boomed the hoist all the way in towards the cabin, grabbed the hoist hook and started lowering the cable. As soon as I had enough slack, I kneeled back down and continued feeding out hoist cable.

I turned to Bob, who was ready and kneeling in the growing puddle just behind me. I handed him the hoist hook, he hooked himself in, disconnected his gunners belt and motioned for me to check him. I checked his hook, tugged on his harness and gave him a firm pat on his shoulder as I moved to the side and out of his way. I sat down and shimmied towards the open cabin door as I took in enough hoist cable to keep it taught. He threw me a thumbs up.

"Rescue check part two," LT Breen said firmly.

"Rescue check part two complete. Ready aft," I said.

I hoisted Bob off the deck and boomed the hoist outward. He dangled just outside the aircraft with his feet propped up on the corner of the cabin deck for stability. He gave me another thumbs up and I started lowering him down.

"Swimmer is at the door. Swimmer is five feet below the aircraft. Swimmer is fifteen feet below the aircraft..."

I continued to paint a picture for the pilots with my words by giving them information every few seconds.

"Swimmer is halfway down."

A huge gust of wind slammed into the aircraft. I whipped my left hand down behind me to keep from getting rolled onto my back. The aircraft rocked sharply to the left and the pilot immediately pushed the cyclic to the right in an attempt to regain a stable hover. In an instant we were back to stable and holding. *Even in a hurricane this man can still hold that hover! Impressive.*

"I have eyes on the swimmer. Swimmer is halfway down."

"Ok. Let's get him on the ground," LCDR Santos said. The aircraft continued to bounce left and right with gusts of wind but LT Breen stabilized and counteracted perfectly.

"Swimmer is twenty feet off the ground. Swimmer is ten feet off the ground. Swimmer is five feet off the ground."

As he lowered, he slowed his swing with his feet until he was firmly on the ground.

"Swimmer is on the ground. Swimmer is disconnecting."

He disconnected the hoist hook and held it directly over his head.

"Swimmer is disconnected, retrieving the hook. Hook is clear of swimmer. Clear back and left," I relayed.

I retrieved the hoist hook as quickly as possible and then closed the cabin door. The cabin almost felt silent without the wind and rain beating in on us.

"Good work, Ashlee," LT Breen said.

"You too, sir," I replied.

I turned to look in the cockpit and checked our fuel state. The wind was so forceful that rainwater now covered the entire inside. Water was dripping down the instrument displays and pooling on the screens in the center console. LCDR Santos found some napkins and proceeded to wipe down the wet surfaces until he held wet wads of paper in his hands. I looked out the cabin window to see Bob running from the house at the end of the cul-de-sac to a neighboring house. He knocked on the door and attempted to open it but it was locked. He ran to the next house. That door was unlocked so he lets himself in. We heard a crackling over the radio.

"6574, this is your swimmer," his transmission was slightly garbled.

"Go ahead," the pilot responded.

"There's no one here. And it doesn't look like anyone in this neighborhood stayed behind."

"All right, are you ready to move on?"

"Yep, let's roll," he said.

LT Breen brought the aircraft to a hover over the same spot. Bob ran outside and positioned himself for the pickup. He stood with his legs wide and slightly bent to keep from getting pushed around by the wind.

I opened the cabin door and the aircraft filled with the loud, howling wind and the rain began to sting my neck. I stood to grab the hoist hook and strapped an extra weight bag to it. I began to lower the hoist hook.

"Hook is at the cabin door. Hook is five feet below the aircraft. Hook is fifteen feet below the aircraft."

I used my free hand to wipe water from my eyes. The visor on my helmet was powerless against the force of the rain.

"Hook is halfway down. Hook is twenty feet off the ground. Hook is ten feet off the ground."

Bob started walking forward to grab the hook. As soon as it was eye level, he grabbed the hook, connected it to the harness and looked up at me with a thumbs up high above his head.

"Swimmer is ready for pick up. Prepare to take the load. Taking the load."

I hoisted him up as quickly as possible, got him in the cabin and closed the sliding cabin door. The howling of the wind was muffled once again as the door closed and locked.

"Alright, a bit anticlimactic, but good work guys. I guess we'll head to the air station now and try getting them on the radio for the next mission."

He nosed the aircraft down and we flew forward. I kept my eyes outside, looking for obstacles and other search and rescue aircraft. The wind was hitting the trees with such force that they bowed over and looked close to breaking. The street lights hanging from wires appeared to dance as they bounced up and down. Everywhere I looked, I saw hazards and obstacles that could turn any standard hoist into a challenge or disaster.

I looked over to my left and scanned the highway we were flying over. Aside from the occasional abandoned car, it was eerily empty and started to flood in certain sections. A flash of color in the distance caught my attention and I leaned closer towards the window. On the highway, an orange blur started to come into sharper focus.

Rising flood waters of Houston

"I think we have company traffic landed on the highway," LCDR Santos.

"Oh wow. Yeah, that's a Coast Guard helicopter."

The helicopter was just sitting on the highway, with the rotor blades running.

"I haven't heard anything on the radio," LT Breen said. "Let's land behind them and see if they need a hand."

He maneuvered the helicopter and landed about a hundred feet behind the other helicopter. It was such an odd feeling landing on a highway with flood waters all around us.

"Eleven o'clock. At the fence," said Bob.

The Hurricane Within

We looked over to our left and could see a small gathering of people behind a building just beyond a chain-link fence that bordered the highway.

"It looks like there's a swimmer on the other side of the fence with some survivors," he continued. "Can I go out there and see if they need a hand, sir?"

"That's a good idea, Bob. Go for it," LCDR Santos said.

He jumped out of the helicopter and started to jog over to the gathering of people. About halfway there, he started to negotiate rapidly rising water. I squinted my eyes and tried to make sense of what was going on by the fence. As best as I could tell, there was a flight mechanic or a pilot on the highway side of the fence, and a swimmer with a small group of survivors on the other side. They were all waist-deep in water. All the while, the helicopter in front continued to run on idle and was radio silent.

"6574, this is your swimmer," we heard over the radio.

"Go ahead."

"We need cable cutters."

"Ashlee, you're up!" LCDR Santos said looking back at me.

"On it, sir." I quickly said. It was a rare opportunity for the flight mechanic to go out in the middle of the action but I didn't hesitate to help. *This was the stuff I only watched in the movies!*

I grabbed the cable cutters, which were usually staged to cut the hoist in the event of an emergency, and after disconnecting from internal communications and my gunners belt, I started jogging to the fence. As I approached the water, I could see that it was moving quickly. I was careful with each of my steps as the water tried to sweep my feet from under me.

I continued wading forward. The water was at my waist, moving quickly and pushing trash, debris, and oil slicks past me. Out of the corner of my eye, I saw a brown blob moving toward me. I turned my head to get a better look. It was about the size of a basketball.

Ants! A giant raft of fire ants were caught up in the flood and floating down the water directly towards me. I tried to jump out of the way, but the flowing water shifted their trajectory and pushed them straight towards me. As the mass got closer to me, I was able to see thousands of fire ants. They were feverishly crawling all over each other as they floated on the water, desperate to find a solid, dry surface. They were just inches from me, I knew I wouldn't be able to jump out of the way and avoid such a large swarm. For a second, I imagined the mass of ants colliding with me, exploding on impact and thousands of ants furiously swarming up my body in a desperate attempt to escape the flood.

Nope! Still clutching the cable cutters in one hand, I pinched my nose with my other hand and threw my body backwards. I took a gasp of air and scanned around me for any more hazardous debris. I continued wading towards the fence and extended my arm to give the cable cutters to my swimmer. Then around the corner the flight mechanic from the other aircraft had made her way to help.

"Hey Kristen!" I shouted. She turned to looked at me with an expression I can only describe as relief and shock, but it seemed my shouting had startled her back into reality. "Good thing I've been working out, huh!" I said with a grin, trying to make her smile, seeing that something had her pretty shaken. With a small chuckle, we looked at each other and quickly got back to the task at hand. That seemed to be just the "Ashlee comedic relief" she needed in the middle of such a chaotic moment.

Taking off from the highway with the elderly survivors as a news crew films.

Graham, the other rescue swimmer from the other crew, was in the water holding up an older woman, while my swimmer, Bob, was with the other woman and an older man. They were all waiting on the other side of the fence and behind a boat connected to its trailer. The older people looked too weak to stand at all, let alone in the waist deep water. One woman was sitting on a walker, with the water line sitting at her chest. She was stoic with tear-filled eyes. The other two women stood still, only betraying their fear with their wide eyes and slack jaws.

I waded over to the two rescue swimmers and noticed they were trying to get around a large boat that was hooked to the trailer. I quickly gathered all my strength to lift the boat up in order to disconnect it from the trailer and make for a shorter exit route to our awaiting helicopter. I helped carry these elderly survivors through the water while the man that could stand went through first, followed by us. Finally, the last woman, who was still sobbing, was helped up from her walker and through the hole.

After helping carry the walker-bound woman up the onramp of the highway, I, the two swimmers, and LCDR Santos helped the remaining four back to my helicopter. They got situated in the aircraft. I helped the woman who was unable to stand into the flight mechanic chair and buckled her in. The other three found a place on the cabin floor.

"That's the one that fell," the swimmer yelled into my ear. I wasn't sure what that meant at that moment, but I thought she seemed okay and I continued getting into the cabin. I hopped in, closed the cabin door, sat on the cabin floor and hooked into the internal communications system.

"On ICS," I said.

"Loud and clear," the pilot responded. "We're heading to the air station. We need fuel." We left our rescue swimmer on scene, allowing us more take-off power and more room in the cabin to fit the survivors.

With that, he pulled power, came to a hover, nosed the aircraft down and we flew away. The other helicopter stayed where it was, sitting alone on the flooded highway.

I turned to face the survivors in the cabin. I was instantly overwhelmed by the smell of urine and feces. Their diapers were soiled. God knows how long they had been sitting in their own excrement. Not wanting to embarrass them, I did my best to make no indication of my sudden awareness that I was sitting in a puddle that their diapers were draining into. I reached out and grabbed the hand of the old lady closest to me. I cupped her hand with both of mine and gave her a reassuring smile. She managed to crack a small smile in return.

I continued to reassure the survivors while I kept a look out for flight hazards. It slowly dawned on me that I was soaked to the bone, sitting in a pool of bio waste, flying in the worst winds with the worst visibility that I had ever encountered and that there was so much more work to do.

First rainy hurricane day at Air Station Houston, Ellington Field, August 27, 2017.

[12] Storm Born

"Semper Paratus"

(Always Ready)

—Motto, U. S. Coast Guard

WE LANDED AT the air station. I was greeted with the friendly faces of people I had worked with in the past and they helped me offload the four elderly survivors. As soon as they were clear of the aircraft, a man in a flight suit ran under the spinning rotor arc with a fuel hose and hooked it up. He ran back outside of the arc and grabbed the dead man stick. I gave him the thumbs up to start fueling. Hot refueling, or refueling an aircraft without shutting it down, was a higher risk evolution that we reserved only for emergencies. It was only worth the risk if we could shave off some time in response to a case.

We had just received word that a woman was stuck in a flooded apartment complex and had gone into labor but was having complications causing her to go in and out of consciousness. We were the only aircraft available to respond. I double checked the security of the fuel cap, hopped into the cabin and strapped into the flight mechanic chair. They gave me a thumbs up. After the hot refueling evolution was complete, we took off to go retrieve our rescue swimmer and head to the pregnant woman in distress.

"Ready aft," I said.

"Alright, let's go," LT Breen said.

We took off to pick up our rescue swimmer who was left at scene by the highway and head to our next case.

"We don't know exactly where we're going," the pilot said. "We just have a general idea so everybody needs to keep a look out."

I looked out around me. The wind was still beating the trees and shaking the power lines. We flew past entire neighborhoods with houses submerged to their roofs, hundreds of cars abandoned on the road, and highways being rapidly swallowed by flood waters. We quickly landed to pick up Bob, who was now accompanied by the rescue swimmer from the other helicopter from the highway and headed off to a series of apartment complexes.

"She's around here somewhere," the LCDR Santos said.

We began to fly in low, slow circles around the apartment buildings. Despite the wind and rain, I chose to open the cabin door so I could hang out the side of the aircraft and get a better view of the ground. After a few passes, I saw a small group of people waving their arms and jumping up and down.

"One o'clock," Bob said.

"I see them," responded LT Breen.

"This area is really flooded, I don't see anywhere to land," LCDR Santos commented.

"I don't either," I agreed.

"What do you guys think?" LCDR Santos asked, directing the question at the crew in the cabin.

"I think we should go down and there and check it out," one of the swimmers suggested.

"Let's get it done" the pilot said.

We came to a hover over a flooded parking lot in front of the building where the people were waving to us. I hoisted one swimmer down. He waded through the water towards the small group of people while I hoisted the second swimmer down. I retrieved the hoist hook and closed the cabin door. The helicopter transitioned from a hover to forward flight and we began to circle the apartment complex as we waited for word from the swimmers.

"We're running low on fuel," LT Breen informed us.

I looked at the instruments and saw that we didn't have too much longer until we would have to return to the air station for more fuel. We continued to circle for another fifteen minutes. I hailed the swimmers on the radio, but nobody responded.

"We have to go," the pilot said. "We'll keep monitoring their frequency and come back."

The Hurricane Within

We broke away from the pattern we had established over the apartment buildings and high-tailed it back to the air station for more fuel. We landed at the air station. The same man that refueled us earlier ran out to hot refuel us again. Another man in a flight suit, a swimmer by the looks of it, ran out with medical gear for infants and loaded it into the cabin. I managed to run inside to use the restroom and make a quick turnaround back to the helicopter. Within a matter minutes, we took off and headed back towards the complex.

"6574, this is your swimmer."

"Go ahead," the LCDR Santos said.

"We have to get her out of here. She's in diabetic shock. She just lost consciousness and the baby is crowning."

"Ok, we obviously can't hoist her then. Is there somewhere we can land?"

"Yeah, the other swimmer found a spot. It's a parking lot about a quarter mile south of the apartment. He's out there now to flag you down."

"Roger, we're about ten minutes out."

We flew as quickly as the aircraft would allow us. Upon reaching the apartment buildings, we quickly spotted the rescue swimmer. He was waving his hands and standing on an island of what used to be a parking lot. Several cars were scattered around with water up to their windows.

The pilot slowed the aircraft down and we started to approach the landing area. I kept one eye outside, and another eye in the cockpit. As we started coming into a hover, the indication for main gearbox torque turned yellow (signaling us to be cautious on the power we were using, not to exceed our maximum allowed). For a split second, it turned red but the pilot quickly nosed the aircraft down and we returned to forward flight.

"We're too heavy," he said.

Our chosen landing area was small and didn't offer much room for error. At our current weight, we weren't able to hover long enough to land safely without over-torqueing the gearbox. At best, over-torqueing the gearbox would force us to take the aircraft out of service for special inspections. At worst, it could cause catastrophic airworthiness failures.

"Let's jettison the fuel and get this woman out of here," said the LCDR Santos.

We flew clear of the landing area and dumped enough fuel to make us light enough to land.

"Let's try this again."

We began another approach to the landing area. As we slowed down, the indication for gearbox torque turned yellow again. We came to a hover over the spit of land. The indication remained yellow. The pilot dropped the collective (a control lever by the left side of the pilot that changes the pitch of the rotary blades) and we touched down.

"Alright, Ashlee. You're up. Take the infant medical gear and meet the swimmers to help. Let them know we don't have much fuel."

"Roger Sir, I'm on it"

I unbuckled and disconnected from the communications system. I had my hands full of infant medical gear. I ran over to the swimmer, who was standing in the water to stay clear of the landing area. He had done an amazing job scouting out a landing area safe for us to land. As I approached him he said, "This way!" We started heading through the water towards an awaiting truck from a good Samaritan who also lived in the apartment complex. We jumped into the bed of the truck and he started plowing through the water. The swimmer said, "You gotta love Texans! Always willing to help!"

The truck pulled up to the building and we hopped off. The commotion from the emergency had created a crowd of onlookers gathered by her apartment building and entryway. "Thank you!" we said to the man in the truck as we jumped off and entered the woman's ground floor apartment.

She was on the couch in bad shape. I ran in, knowing that our fuel load was low and if we did not get this woman out, there was a good chance she and her baby would not make it. I shouted to the husband, "Sir we need to get your wife out of here NOW or she isn't going to make it." With that sense of urgency reinstalled into the moment, we began to get blankets prepared to carry her out to the waiting truck to take us back to the helicopter. At this point there was an even larger crowd gathered from the apartments around us. Bob held onto my vest for dear life so I didn't fall out as we both sat on the edge of the crowded truck bed.

"She's going unconscious again," the swimmer stated with a hint of alarm in his voice.

The husband and I started grabbing blankets and ran to the truck that was still waiting outside. We tossed the blankets in the bed of the truck. The two rescue swimmers and I carried the woman out to the truck. They carefully placed the woman in the bed of the truck. One of the swimmers continued to aid the woman. She had regained consciousness but did not seem coherent. The husband and I tried to hold a blanket over her to keep the rain away.

The other swimmer and I kneeled on the side of the truck holding on for dear life as we drove back towards the helicopter. As soon as we were close, I rushed to the helicopter and began to rip all the spare equipment out of the cabin. I pulled out the life raft, the basket, the rescue strops, the trail lines and all of the other unnecessary SAR gear.

Within minutes, the pregnant woman was carried by both the swimmers and loaded onto the aircraft. The husband and Bob boarded the aircraft. The other swimmer and I jogged away from the helicopter and gave the pilot a thumbs up when we were clear of the rotor arc. The remaining swimmer and I linked arms and stared up in awe as the helicopter pulled into a hover and flew off towards the hospital.

I walked over to the SAR gear. I took a seat on the life raft and closed my eyes. The rush of silence kicked in. I took advantage of the unexpected break to allow myself a moment of calmness in the midst of chaos and said a prayer. The swimmer and I had a moment of release and spoke about what had just happened and the earlier events from the highway. That deep personal moment we had certainly helped me decompress a bit. He also told me why his helicopter was on the highway. I had no idea their hoist cable inadvertently made contact with a power line with a survivor in the basket. *Wow. Thank God everyone was okay.*

After a short period, the helicopter returned to get us and we headed back to home base, Air Station Houston, Ellington field. Once the engines shut down and the debrief was completed, I walked around, suddenly exhausted, trying to find a place to sleep. I found a spare room with a couch and table.

The Hurricane Within

I found my friend and pilot from another crew, Emily. We crouched in the room she had found and debriefed about our crazy days of flying. It was these little moments of relief that made the stress decrease. For that I was thankful.

Shortly after having a long talk with a rescue swimmer from earlier in the day, I hung up my wet and biohazard-filled flight suit to dry, wrung out my socks, and prayed my boots would be dry for the following day. Little did we know we had flown over eight hours that day with barely stopping to eat or drink. Those things seemed irrelevant when there are people struggling to avoid certain death, and you're the one who can save them.

[13] My New Crew

"But they who wait for the Lord shall renew their strength; they shall mount up with wings like the eagles; they shall run and not be weary; they shall walk and not faint."

— Isaiah 40:31

I WOKE TO that familiar ring tone. *Where am I?* Completely disoriented, I looked over at the clock on the wall to my left. It was 0400. I had managed to squeeze in a few hours of sleep after getting back to the air station late the night before. I swung my legs off the makeshift bed and cradled my head in my hands. People were sleeping wherever they could find a space that was out of the way. Coasties gathered in Houston in droves without any options for lodging. People were sleeping on the floor, on every available couch, even propped up against SAR equipment. I managed to find an unoccupied coffee table and couch in the FBO (private

The Hurricane Within

airport service station) next to the air station. It kept me off the floor, which was crawling with bugs looking for a dry place to hide. I slept like a rock.

I got up, wearing the fresh undershirt and shorts I had packed, and collected my flight suit and boots. They failed to dry out like I was hoping but I was able to put on dry socks. I got goosebumps on my arms as I slid into the cold and wet flight suit. I glanced at the bottom of my feet and they were still wrinkled from being waterlogged in wet boots for over nine hours.

I made my way over to the hangar. Dozens of other people were already up, some hadn't slept at all. Nobody was standing still. Everyone was launching aircraft, fueling, inspecting, or preparing for a flight. I looked around for someone in charge and could tell me where to go, but everyone was actively working. The place was now buzzing with many more search and rescue assets than the day before. The weather looked even worse.

I heard the familiar sound of an MH-65 (helicopter) on final approach. I turned to watch the aircraft land. I looked over at the fuel pits and saw that one was already being used to hot refuel a helicopter. The helicopter that just landed started taxiing to the second fuel pit, which was empty and unmanned. I grabbed a cranial (protective safety gear for your head required to wear during hot refueling operations) and ran over to the unmanned fuel pit and prepped it for use. The helicopter taxied into the pit, whipping the heavy rain about and into my face. The flight mechanic jumped out of the helicopter, installed the chocks, opened the fuel panel and gave me a thumbs up. I swung the thick fuel hose over my shoulder, leaned forward, and ran the fuel hose towards the aircraft. I connected it to the helicopter, ran back and grabbed the dead man stick. With a signal from the flight mechanic, I started to send fuel to the aircraft.

The rain continued to fall heavily. My clothes quickly become soaked again. Raindrops collected on my eyelashes, making it difficult to see. As I continued to fuel, I found a small box labeled "PPE" by the fuel hose reel. I opened it and considered myself lucky to find some safety goggles. I put them on and they helped.

The flight mechanic gave the cut throat signal and I stopped fueling. I ran back under the rotor arc, disconnected the hose and ran in back. I started to reel the hose back in but changed my mind when I saw another helicopter landing. As soon as the helicopter left the fuel pit, another helicopter taxied in and took its place. As with the last helicopter, a flight mechanic hopped out, installed the chocks, opened the fuel panel and gave me a thumbs up. I ran in, connected the fuel hose, manned the dead man stick, and disconnected the fuel hose.

Before I knew it, I found myself in a trance-like state as I performed the same task over and over while listening to the monotonous hum of helicopters. My sense of time passing quickly dissipated. The helicopters came in one after another. They were all hungry for fuel and desperate to get back in the air. As far as I could tell, there were about a dozen coming in and out. I teamed up with another stellar flight mechanic named Ryan Beard, and the two of us would swap out every hour or so to give each other a quick bathroom break and a chance to hunt down a granola bar. Every so often I would find myself helping with aircraft inspections or troubleshooting avionics discrepancies.

The Hurricane Within

By now air stations all over were sending aircraft and crews to help out with the rescues. Every now and then, the monotony would break when a flight mechanic I recognized hopped out of an aircraft. "Troy Ramsdell!" I shouted and ran over for a quick hug and small talk. Troy was one of my best buddies and rescue swimmers that I helped train and then in turn flew many hours with. "Mari Delong!" I said with a big smile and a wave. I was in training school with Mari many years back. "LT Pelkey!" Her eyes beamed back with a smile as she loaded up her helicopter for departure. I worked with her husband, Dan who was an AET in Detroit with me. One of my friends and mentors. "Nick McConnell!" He pointed at me with a look of surprise and gave me a big smile and a head nod. Nick and I were stationed together in Detroit and had flown together on several occasions. The silver lining to this hectic and chaotic operation was the small reunion that began to unfold with some of the most amazing people I had worked with in the past. As we stood there waiting for the fuel to transfer, we signaled to each other about the intensity of the rain.

After disconnecting the hose from another aircraft and snaking it out in front of the hose reel, I looked over and saw someone running towards me. He wasn't in a flight suit, so I assumed he was an airman. "You're wanted inside!" he said. "I've been told to take over."

"You're going to want these," I took the safety goggles off and handed them to him. I jogged back into the hangar. I paused in the center of the hangar and looked around for whoever called for me. A puddle of water started to collect around my boots. The sensation of not being rained on felt suddenly strange. It almost felt like walking on dry land after being on a boat. I looked around to find a clock. I still felt as though I just woke up.

"Hey!" I spun around and saw a flight mechanic walking towards me.

"Are you the one that wants me?" I asked him.

"Yeah, I'm getting put on heavy maintenance. Your clock is reset, right?" he asked, referring to the mandatory "rest time" required of me after yesterday's flights. "You want to take my flight?"

"Hell Yeah, I can take it," I said. "Is there somewhere I can get some food?"

He pointed to maintenance control, the main brains of the engineering department. I walked over to Chief Jamison who was a mentor and a supervisor from New Orleans who had also been a flight mechanic during Hurricane Katrina (now the author of the Afterword to this book). He was immersed with the maintenance logbooks and glanced up at me.

"Hey Ash, how you holding up?" he said.

"I'm beat, chief. I'm starting to feel the adrenaline seep out of my body and the reality is setting in on how tired I am."

He looked over at me with a big smile and said, "They need you, girl. Put your game face on and go grab a Red Bull under Senior Chief's desk and fly safe." In that quick instance, those words hit me hard. *THEY NEED ME*. I Roger'd up, grabbed a Red Bull, and walked out to find my flight crew. It was going to be a long night, I thought.

The Hurricane Within

I FOUND MY new crew. They were a mix of pilots and rescue swimmers from various units. I sat down with a half-eaten granola bar to listen to the brief. I didn't recognize either of the pilots, but they were very welcoming and extremely focused on the mission ahead. LT JJ Briggs and LT Bukata were signing out the helicopter in maintenance control. The pilot explained that the hurricane had settled over Houston and the weather was even worse than the day before.

I was thrilled to see that Troy Ramsdell, one of my best buddies, was my rescue swimmer. Finally, some comforting news. I felt at ease flying with Troy, with whom I'd flown many times before in Detroit. I was stoked! Troy and I became great friends in Detroit. He was a ladies man, so much so that he even deemed the nickname, "Angel Eyes." His piercing blue eyes would steal many hearts of young women everywhere. To me, he was sort of a little brother whom I had helped train. I couldn't be more excited to fly again with my bro.

Ashlee Leppert

AST2 Troy Ramsdell and I, August 28, 2017

[14] The Cross

"Life is wasted if we do not grasp the glory of the cross, cherish it for the treasure that it is, and cleave to it as the highest price of every pleasure and the deepest comfort in every pain."

—John Piper

THE PILOTS BEGAN the brief. "It's Coast Guard VFR," he joked, referring to Visual Flight Rules, which are only for clear skies. "We'll stick our nose in it and see how we feel. Logistics aren't particularly organized yet, so we're simply going to fly to Beaumont. Beaumont is experiencing intense flooding so we'll take a look around. If we pick anyone up, we're going to drop them off at the convention center instead of bringing them back here. They've set up a shelter there. Anyone have any questions?" I was still chewing on the granola bar, so I simply shook my head no. We suited up and departed the air station within minutes of completing the brief.

The pilot was correct, the weather was even worse than the day before. I hadn't felt it when I was on the ground fueling the aircraft, but I could feel it in the helicopter. My bladder was full and I was instantly reminded of this as the gusts of wind tossed the light aircraft around as we flew forward. *Rookie move forgetting to pee before takeoff. Ugh.* Rain managed to find its way into the cabin despite the doors being shut. The world around us was various shades of gray and white. Less than 300 feet of ceilings and at least 45 knots of gusts or more. All along the horizon there were glimpse of other rescue aircraft. It was an ominous, almost apocalyptic sight to behold.

"Alright, we're over Beaumont," the LT Briggs said. "Keep your eyes out for anyone that looks like they need help."

I moved my seat closer to the cabin door and looked out the window, searching for anything that might be a sign of distress. The area was alive with the sharp movement of trees, blowing debris and whipping rain. As far as I could see, the town was saturated with power lines, trees and other tall structures.

As my eyes scanned over a group of buildings, I saw a man run out, waving his arms frantically. Two more people ran out behind him and started to do the same.

"3 o'clock," I said. "There's people waving at us."

"In sight," the LT Bukata said.

The pilot circled back around to approach the small group of people that had gathered to flag us down.

"There's nowhere to land, and there are powerlines on the right side of the building," LT Briggs warned.

"In sight," a focused LT Bukata replied. "With our nose in the wind, they'll be behind us. Ashlee, keep an eye on those powerlines and make sure we don't drift."

"Yes, sir."

"We'll drop the swimmer to assess the situation and take it from there. We're only going to hoist those in critical condition."

We came to a hover near the group of people. The size of the group had doubled. A few were still waving their hands, apparently not wanting to risk any chance of losing our attention. The others huddled together in a futile attempt to shield themselves from the rain.

I opened the cabin door and felt the now familiar sensation of wind and rain rushing into the cabin. I stood up, boomed the hoist in and then lowered enough cable for the swimmer to hook in. He hooked in and, after I double-checked his harness, he scooted forward to the cabin door and swung his legs over the side. I pulled in the slack on the cable until he was dangling in front of me. I boomed the hoist back out and with a thumbs up from the swimmer, I began to lower him carefully, keeping the pilots in a position that wouldn't place him in a tree, rooftop or powerlines, all of which were in a 10-foot square radius below. Meanwhile, I had rain whipping at my face causing a blinding sting which added another layer of stress.

"Swimmer is at the door. Swimmer is below the aircraft. Position and altitude are good. Swimmer is halfway down. Swimmer is ten feet off the ground. Swimmer is on the ground. Swimmer is disconnecting. Retrieving hoist hook. Hook is ten feet off the ground. Swimmer walking towards the survivors. Hoist hook is at the door."

The wind continued to push our aircraft about but the pilot, LT Bukata was doing an incredible job of keeping it relatively steady. I sat at the door and watched as the swimmer approached the group and began to talk to them. I watched him pull out his radio and speak into it, but I didn't hear anything on our end. I turned around to check my communications controls, but everything looked as it should.

I looked back down to see the swimmer holding his radio above his head with one hand and pointing at it with the other. I made an exaggerated motion, tapping the part of the helmet that covered my ear and then shrugging. He put his radio back in his harness and then threw his hands up in the air, creating half a rectangle with his arm, which was the hand signal for the rescue basket.

"Swimmer is calling for a basket pick up," I told the pilots. "His radio isn't working."

"Start the rescue checklist for the basket recovery of a survivor," LT Briggs responded.

I started the checklist and grabbed the basket. I hooked it to the hoist, lowered it down, and placed it about twenty feet in front of the swimmer. The swimmer walked towards the basket with a man. The man was able-bodied enough to get in the basket on his own and when he was settled, the swimmer gave me a thumbs up.

"Ready for pick up. Prepare to take the load," I said as I took in cable slack and began to lift the basket off of the ground. The swimmer continued to hold the basket, steadying it as long as he could while I lifted it towards the aircraft.

"Survivor is ten feet off the ground. Position and altitude are good. Survivor is…"

"Ashlee, keep talking," the pilot said. His voice was concerned.

"Survivor is halfway…"

"Ashlee, you need to keep talking," his voice grew stern.

I suddenly realized that I wasn't hearing my own words in my headset, which was an indication that I wasn't transmitting anything over the internal communications system. I pushed the button hooked to my vest that allowed me to manually transmit, but nothing changed. I leaned forward, closer to the pilot, and I continued to hoist while yelling as loud as I could.

"SURVIVOR IS HALFWAY UP. SURVIVOR IS TEN FEET BELOW THE AIRCRAFT. ALTITUDE AND POS…" my voice suddenly screamed through the internal communications system, causing the pilot to jump.

"Survivor is at the door. Booming in basket."

I pulled the basket into the helicopter and helped the man out. He was holding a child. I quickly helped them into the cabin and then looked over my shoulder to see the rescue swimmer giving the hand signal for the basket again.

"Swimmer is requesting the basket," I said.

"Start rescue checklist for delivery of basket to swimmer," the pilot said. "If you lose comms again, just do what you did last hoist."

I lowered the basket down and landed it on the same spot as before. This time, a young woman holding a small child got into the basket. The swimmer gave me the thumbs up after she was settled and I hoisted her up towards the helicopter. My communications system failed shortly after she was hoisted off the ground, but I was able to quickly identify the problem through troubleshooting and continue hoisting until it came back online.

As I pulled the young woman with her child into the helicopter, I could see the look of terror in her eyes. Her gaze was fixed on the child and partially hidden behind the wet hair that stuck to her face. The child was wailing so loudly that I could hear it over the noise of the helicopter and the hurricane. She gripped the child tightly to her chest as I pushed the basket to the back of the helicopter. After a few more hoists the cabin was packed with cold and frightened bodies.

"We're running low on fuel," LT Briggs said. "We're going to have to leave the swimmer on scene and come back."

I leaned out the cabin door to signal to the swimmer that we needed fuel. I closed the door and we transitioned from a hover to forward flight. I turned around to check on the survivors. The woman was still sitting in the rescue basket and trying desperately to calm her child. Her whole body was shaking as she rocked back and forth and ran her hand over her child's head. We locked eyes for a moment. I mouthed the words "Everything is going to be okay," and gave her a reassuring smile. That seemed to calm her nerves a little.

We landed at the convention center and dropped them off. A small group of volunteers were waiting outside to assist the inbound helicopters with the survivors. As the man exited the aircraft, he shook my hand. The woman breezed past me in a frantic hurry and ran to the nearest volunteer. She said something to them that incited a sense of urgency and they began to rush her and her child inside.

The Hurricane Within

Once everyone was offloaded and as soon as the area was clear, we departed the convention center and flew to the air station for fuel. Helicopters lined the highway. Eager to recover our swimmer, we were happy to see that the hot refueling operations were still running like clockwork. The crew manning the fuel pits turned us around expeditiously and we headed back to the location where we left the swimmer.

As we flew forward, I scanned the airspace around us for company traffic and other flight hazards. It dawned on me that I had become unsettlingly comfortable with the severe weather. The roar of the wind and the pounding of the rain had become like white noise. The weather was worsening and what little visibility we had before was quickly dissipating.

"6516, this is your swimmer," a voice broke through and cackled over the radio. I felt a sense of relief that he had gotten his radio to work.

"Swimmer, 6516, Go ahead," LT Briggs replied.

"I have a lot of babies and small children with health issues that need to be evacuated. Requesting the basket as soon as you're back on scene."

"Understood, requesting basket," he said over the radio. And then to me, "Start rescue checklist for basket recovery of survivors. We're are only about 10 mics now."

Flying back out there and scanning the horizon, I became very aware of the danger we were in. I made peace with the fact that I may not make it home, and I was okay with that. After all, this is what serving your country is all about. In that moment of acceptance, I gazed out the window. In the distance, the fog and rain suddenly parted and there, amidst the storm, standing strong against the violent winds and thrashing

135

rains, stood a massive cross. Its brilliant white shade made it shine in contrast to the gray, menacing scene that surrounded it. An instant feeling of protection blanketed me and I felt the presence of the Lord comfort me and renew my strength.

The giant cross that comforted me in the middle of the hurricane rescues, Sagemont Church in Houston, August 28, 2017.

[15] The Basket

"Carry each other's burdens, and in this way you will fulfill the law of Christ."

—Galatians 6:2

I BEGAN MY checklist and was ready to start hoisting as soon as we were on scene. My nerves were on high alert. We came into a hover near the group of survivors that had gathered around the rescue swimmer. I hung out the side of the helicopter to get a good visual on the swimmer. Through the thick rain, I could make out several trees that were fairly close to the pickup point, which would give us little room for error.

"Ready aft for basket delivery to survivors," I said.

"Ready aft for basket delivery, aye," LT Bukata said. "Keep a close eye on those trees."

Ashlee Leppert

"In sight. Booming out basket."

As I lowered the basket, the wind and rain hit the helicopter with great force. If it weren't for the steady hands of my pilots, the aircraft would have been bounced around like a ping pong ball. He counteracted the forces of Mother Nature with such diligence that my basket only experienced a gentle swing as it made its way down. Once the basket was on the deck, the swimmer helped what appeared to be a mother and child into it. With a thumbs up from the swimmer, we began our first live hoist from this group.

"Prepare to take the load. Taking the load," I reported. My eyes darted between the basket and the trees, making sure we didn't come close to hitting any flight hazards. I hoisted them up as quickly as I could. Once the mother and child were at the door of the cabin, I boomed them in and directed them to get out of the basket and sit in the back of the helicopter. I immediately boomed the basket back out in preparation for the next hoist as the pilot expertly steadied the hover. I delivered the basket to the swimmer. This time, a father and child were assisted into the basket. I hoisted them into the cabin and directed them to sit next to mother and child that were hoisted before them.

I immediately boomed the basket out again. I delivered it to the swimmer. A woman was helped into the basket. As I got her into the helicopter, I could see she was significantly shaken, more so than the last four survivors. She sat in the basket with her head between her knees and her hands laced behind her head. She ignored my gestures to get out of the basket and continued to sit there, rocking back and forth. With the help of the two other adults in the cabin, we were able to pry her out of the basket and into the back of the cabin.

"We just lost GPS 2," the pilot said calmly over the radio. "Nothing serious but we'll make a note of it. Shit, and we keep getting a heading failure."

"All the water intrusion is starting to affect our avionics," LT Briggs noted.

"We'll keep hoisting, but if it gets worse, we'll have to abort," he added.

"Roger, sir" I said.

I boomed the basket back out and delivered it back to the swimmer. He helped a small boy into the basket. I hoisted him up and as I was pulling him into the cabin, I could see that his legs were shaking so violently that his little knees were knocking together. I picked him up and placed him on the flight mechanic seat behind me. I turned around and delivered the basket again. This time, another mother and child got in and I hoisted them up. They joined the group of survivors huddled together in the back of the cabin. The altitude being 120 feet or so, the gusts of wind, the tree tops whipping around, all made for a dangerous scenario.

"We're running low on fuel. We only have enough for one more hoist," LT Briggs said keeping his eyes scanning the aircraft components and other "safety pilot duties." I looked down at the swimmer and he signaled that he understood the radio transmission and was ready for the basket again. I hoisted the basket back down to the swimmer. First, he helped a woman into the basket. Then he started putting things into the basket with her. I squinted my eyes in an attempt to see what he was loading through the thick rain. It appeared to be bundles of clothes.

"What the hell," I thought to myself. "We're low on fuel! She doesn't need her stuff."

The swimmer placed several more bundles into the basket and finally gave me the pickup signal. Confused, but trusting Troy and his reasoning, I hoisted the woman and her baggage up to the helicopter. I simply pushed the basket into the cabin and directed her to stay put.

"That's everyone," I told the pilots. "Just the swimmer is left."

"Ok, we have just enough fuel to pick him up with a bare hook recovery."

I disconnected the hook from the basket and hoisted it down to the swimmer. He hooked in almost as soon as he got the cable in his hands and gave me a thumbs up. I hoisted him up until he was dangling just outside of the cabin door. I looked behind me to figure out where he should go, only to realize that the cabin was so full that I was being pushed to the doors edge myself.

"There's barely anymore more room," I told the pilots.

"He's going to have to squeeze by the door," the pilot responded, "and Ash just grab a hold of his harness and leave the door open. Make sure he is secure."

"Roger." I grabbed his arms and locked them into mine as I knelt on the cabin floor.

The swimmer propped his feet onto the edge of the cabin floor, spread his arms across the span of the opening. The nose of the aircraft dipped slightly as we transitioned to a forward flight and we began to bee line it to the convention center. I turned around to check on all of the survivors. I had placed a young boy in my seat who must have been only 5 or 6 years old. He was alone and terrified wearing nothing but a t-shirt and shorts. His thin little legs were shaking uncontrollably. I looked at him and spoke loudly so he could hear me over the roar of the storm. "You are sitting in the best seat in the house!" I gave him a big smile and I grabbed his hand to comfort him. I placed a survival blanket over his trembling legs. This small gesture seemed to ease his mind. My attention quickly turned to the rest of my survivors.

The woman in the basket was leaning forward, trying to grab a yellow bundle by her feet. I leaned over to see that she was reaching for a rain jacket but was unable to grasp it because of the large bundles she was holding against her chest and in her lap. I reached toward the yellow bundle and started to lift the edge of the jacket, revealing the unmistakable color of flesh. I pulled the fabric back further to reveal a tiny face peering up at me. It was a beautiful baby boy. His sparse, light hair was wet and glued to his forehead and his diaper was bloated, but he didn't seem to mind his adverse environment. He was still, and stared up at me with large, pensive eyes. I reached down to touch his head but he grabbed my hand first. He wrapped his tiny hand around two of my fingers and squeezed. His face lit up with the type of wide-eyed excitement that only the innocence of children could produce.

I looked up from the excited baby to see the woman in the basket carefully inspecting the rest of her belongings. There were three more bundles in her lap. Each was a balled-up mass of soaking wet jackets and blankets. She carefully picked up one of the bundles and placed it against her left shoulder. She pulled back a flap of wet fabric just enough to reveal a second baby with thick, black hair hidden underneath. Two bundles remained. With her one free hand, she scooped up the third bundle and propped it against her right shoulder. Yet another baby was swaddled within. This one was flailing so much that he pushed the fabric off himself.

After she secured the two babies on her shoulders and the one smiling baby nestled at her feet, she checked on the bundle that was still on her lap. My heart sank as I realized how still this last remaining bundle was. If there was a fourth baby inside, I would think it would be kicking and squirming like the others. She pealed back the jacket to reveal another little body lying face down and motionless. Panic set in instantly as I was certain something was horribly wrong. Quickly I grabbed the baby and gave him a quick pat on the behind to induce a response. Troy immediately noticed my panic and carefully took the baby into his arms. Within seconds his beautiful brown eyes were open and a cry let out. *Thank you God,* I thought. We wrapped the child back up and secured in the basket.

I looked around at the babies. For a brief moment, all four sets of tiny, helpless eyes were staring up at me simultaneously. I had just mistaken these little souls for bags of clothes that should be left behind in the flood waters. So often I would find myself just going through the motions as I hoisted survivors. As I took in this scene, I became overwhelmed with a sense of purpose. I was reminded of the vital impact that all search and rescue operators have, and the importance of every soul aboard this helicopter. That vision will forever be burned into my memory.

I turned to look at Troy. He was pointing at the various survivors and appeared to be counting them. Behind him, I could see we were approaching the convention center.

The Hurricane Within

Although I was exhausted, it was still hard to believe that we had already been flying for close to three hours. We landed at the convention center. It felt very strange landing on the middle of a highway, but watching the other rescue aircraft, it seemed to be running like clockwork. The survivors started to push forward as soon as we were on the ground, so I had to motion for them to remain where they were for a moment longer.

When it was safe for them to exit, Troy and I helped all of the survivors out of the helicopter and into the care of Red Cross personnel. Despite the urgency to get out of the rain and seek out medical attention, one of the mothers stopped to give each of us a hug.

As the truck departed, I turned and looked at Troy, "that was a pretty crazy one," I said.

"Yeah, it was. I think we might have broken a record."

"What do you mean?"

"Including our crew, all the survivors and those babies, we managed to squeeze seventeen people into this tiny helicopter."

My mind began to wonder as we taxied onto the packed runway back at our temporary home, Ellington Field Houston. Those fleeting moments of looking into the eyes of each one of my survivors will forever be ingrained into my mind. Each life-changing journey began together as quickly as it ended. *What were their names? Who were their families? What was their favorite song?* The sad reality is, I will never know. In the scariest moments of their lives they will only remember me as the rain-soaked female flight mechanic with a warm, welcoming smile on her face that non-verbally conveys, *You are safe now. I won't let anything happen to you.*

I hope they will never forget my face because Lord knows, I won't ever forget theirs.

[16] Water Intrusion

"You are the light of the world. A city set on a hill cannot be hidden. Nor do people light a lamp and put it under a basket, but on a stand, and it gives light to all in the house. In the same way, let your light shine before others, so that they may see your good works and give glory to you Father who is in heaven."

—Matthew 5:14-16

I WOKE UP on the third day feeling an odd mixture of refreshed and utterly exhausted. After bagging out the day before, we learned that someone had managed to procure motel rooms for us near the air station. We would be able to take off our wet clothes, take hot showers, and sleep in real beds instead of fighting each other for floor space. Getting to the motel was an adventure in itself. We used a government vehicle to load up the truck with as many people as we could, including their gear. We expertly navigated the side streets as well as on-ramps and parking lots to finally arrive at the hotel, one of the few structures left that wasn't completely under water. A pilot from earlier had gotten their rental vehicle stuck in the flood waters. So we knew it was like a jungle out there. We all laughed about how he should stick to flying helicopters and leave the driving up to the mechanics. All the roads were still terribly flooded. Abandoned vehicles were scattered all around us. Homes and buildings were almost completely submerged. It was difficult to imagine this area was once a bustling city full of life. It felt like an underwater graveyard.

Upon arrival at the motel, the first thing I did was take a shower. The hot water soothed the chill that had taken over, but the real pleasure was drying off. As I ran the towel across my body, I took a long look at myself. I studied my wrinkled and waterlogged skin. The bottom of my feet had become so pruned and saturated that my skin was starting to peel off. *Gross*, I thought.

Dry for the first time in days, I pulled out my cell phone. Surprisingly, it still worked after being in my soaked flight suit pocket. I took this moment to call my mother. For the first time since the rescues began, I was able to decompress. I tried to hold it in and be strong but just like at my father's funeral, I broke down. I sobbed into the phone with my mother barely making out my words.

"Mom, there are just *so* many people who need help, this is devastating." The conversation was just the release I needed. My mom calmed me down and reminded me that we're all doing the best we could. "God will protect you, honey. You're a hero, baby girl."

My eyes were so heavy and my body yearned for rest, but I still struggled to fall into sleep straight away. My mind kept wandering to all of the survivors I had picked up in the last few days and to the four small babies, with their frightened eyes staring at me. For the first hour, as soon as I felt myself drifting off, I would abruptly wake back up with a surge of energy. I would become overwhelmed with the urge to get back to work and to do something. I had to consciously remind myself that I was grounded and was mandated to rest. Eventually, my body overtook me and I drifted away into a dreamless, heavy sleep.

We made our way to the air station at first light. I knew I would not be flying because a group of fresh flight mechanics had arrived the day before, so I decided to find someone that looked like they were in charge of maintenance.

"Where do you need me, chief?" I asked. He tossed a roll of silver tape at me. It was hundred-mile-an-hour tape, which is like thick aluminum foil with a sticky side.

"Start taping up all the seams on the exterior avionics rack panel," he directed. "Water intrusion is out of control. Every single one of these planes is having avionics issues. Hell, one aircraft lost pitch trim, autopilot 2 and both VOR's."

"You got it," I replied. "My aircraft yesterday was having all sorts of problems. We kept losing internal comms. I had to scream my hoist commands at the pilot. Thankfully I had that can of avionics cleaner with me to blast out the water intrusion in my mic." Good ol' tweet-in-a-can, as we called it.

"You and everyone else. I've been flying in shit weather for over a decade. I've never seen the aircraft have this many problems. Come find me when you're done and we'll put you on something else."

I turned around and found the nearest aircraft. The exterior avionics rack panel was on the outside-left side of the helicopter. It was a large panel that spanned the length of my arms. All of the panels had a rubber gasket that proved to be ineffective against the monstrous winds and rains of Hurricane Harvey. I began to apply the thick, metal tape to the panel's edge, being careful to rub the tape thoroughly to ensure a proper seal. I looked over to see another girl applying tape to the exterior of the aircraft. It was my friend Kristen from New Orleans, the same girl I had seen the first day on the highway helping the group of elderly survivors and looking like she had seen a ghost.

"Hey Kristen!" I yelled across the hangar. She turned abruptly and gave me a quirky half smile and waved. She began to walk towards me and as she got closer, I could see she did not look as flustered as she did the other day. She gave me a quick hug and then we began to apply tape on the aircraft together.

"How have you been?" I asked her. "You looked really shocked the last time I saw you."

She nodded in agreement. "I thought we had just killed someone."

"What?"

"You didn't hear how we lost our hoist?" she asked.

"It's been go, go, go since the second we flew on scene. I've barely had time to talk to anyone," I said.

"Those older people at the fence," she said, "we started to hoist them. I had one of the women in the basket and started to hoist her up, but the aircraft started drifting to the right. I told the pilot the aircraft was drifting left and I tried to con him back right, but he didn't hear me because of my ICS having water intrusion." We finished taping up the aircraft we were working on and moved onto another helicopter as she continued her story. "I lost internal comms," she continued. "I guess all the rain had gotten into my mic. Anyways, we started drifting dangerously close to a power line. The pilot couldn't hear my conning commands, then it hit me that I couldn't hear my own voice in my headset and I knew he wasn't hearing anything from me either. The woman was being lifted out of the water when we drifted right and hit a power line that parted the cable."

"I just saw a flash of bright light that severed the cable and the basket began to fall. She fell at least fifteen or twenty feet. I mean, at least they were in waist deep water when we grabbed them, so that probably helped. But I thought she was dead. I thought she was too old to survive something like that."

"Oh my God," I said.

"Yeah. So we landed on the highway and the swimmer came up with the plan to help transport the survivors through the fence and onto the helicopter. That's when you guys showed up."

"Wow, I had no idea. We just saw company traffic sitting on the highway and decided to check it out."

"It's a good thing you did. We obviously needed help."

I assured her, "Well it's like the Wild Wild West out here. We're all dealing with crazy scenarios. Keep your head up, she is alive and okay. You did a great job, girl!" Then I gave her another hug.

We finished taping up all the aircraft, so I found the chief for another job. I didn't fly that day, but I kept busy until well past midnight doing anything I could to help get aircraft back in the air as soon as possible. I assisted with refueling operations, I performed maintenance inspections and I ran back and forth between aircraft and the hangar to retrieve any requested survival equipment. The work was endless and I found myself scrambling about with little time to rest. When I got hungry, I simply crushed down a granola bar. Despite the constant activity, the work was therapeutic and gave me an opportunity to rest from the stress that came with flying search and rescue.

It was during this time that I had a moment to actually watch the flawless marching of the ants on the hanger deck working hour after hour to keep these aircraft flying. For every flight hour there are about 20 maintenance hours required to keep the aircraft functioning—*20 maintenance hours*! We were pressing these aircraft to the maximum. People taking care of people. Whether you were out there doing routine inspections, fueling the aircraft, or flying and pulling people out of the water, every job mattered.

Throughout the day I would be greeted with another familiar face that I had worked with in the past, including pilots I had flown with in Detroit, or mechanics that I went to training school with, and even a senior chief who I was stationed with in Puerto Rico almost eight years earlier. These people were my Coast Guard family. The quick hugs and small conversations reminiscing about the old made the days enjoyable.

AET2 Mari Delong, myself, AMT3 Kristen Blackledge, Air Station Houston, August 29, 2017.

[17] My Final Hoist

"Have I not commanded you? Be strong and courageous. Do not be afraid; do not be discouraged, for the Lord your God will be with you wherever you go."

—Joshua 1:9

A S I WALKED to the hangar on my fourth day in Houston, I was pleased to find that the weather wasn't nearly as severe. The sun wasn't out, but the rain had subsided and the wind wasn't as violent as it had been. Word was spreading that the flood waters had not receded though, and many people were still in need of help. My first thought was that search and rescue operations would die down a bit since the weather was no longer posing an immediate threat to anyone. But then the realization creeped into my head that people that still required evacuation had been waiting days for assistance. Any remaining survivors with medical conditions would be in critical need of help.

Upon arrival, I opened up ALMIS (a computer program that houses all of the aircraft maintenance history and flight schedules with the crews and departure times). I saw my name and scrolled down to view my crew. Nate Feske was my rescue swimmer? Hell yea! My long-time buddy from Detroit was sent down here for operations. What an exciting feeling that we would be flying together. I set off to locate my crew for a brief.

"Good morning!" I said as I entered the room.

"ASHLEE!" Nates energy matched my excitement to see him.

I didn't recognize either of the pilots but they both stood up to shake my hand and introduce themselves. They were both young and, given their junior rank, probably brand new to Coast Guard aviation.

Neighborhoods underwater.

"Alright," LT Thornton began the brief. "Nice to meet you all! Let's get to briefing. Everyone here has been flying since day one, right?"

We all nodded our heads.

"Okay. Today will be a little bit different. It was kind of like the Wild West the first few days, but now there are a lot of high ranking hands in the pot so our operations are going to be a lot more structured. We're getting ordered to fly specific search patterns and what not. From what I hear, we haven't been having too many problems with our avionics since the rain has subsided, but we'll keep an eye on that. And let's make sure we're looking out for power lines, trees, and other flight hazards. We're grabbing the next helicopter that a crew bags out of. Anyone have any questions?"

We all shook our heads and I responded with, "No sir, sounds like a plan."

"Alright, we'll likely fly until we bag out, so make sure you throw some snacks in your helmet bags. I'll see you guys at the plane."

We all left the brief and went our separate ways to collect our flight gear and handle any last-minute personal business. After a pre-flight inspection and a start of the engines, we were airborne and heading to the start of our search pattern.

The flight there felt so smooth and we were finally able to see more than just the gray haze of the obstacles immediately in front of us. As we buzzed along, I looked out and got my first real view of Houston. The roads and cars were under water, trees had been uprooted, and houses had been destroyed. Despite the chaos of the scene below, it was eerily quiet and still, with no sign of movement or life. Everyone once in a while I would see a dead horse floating or cattle squeezed tight onto the only dry patch of grass. Dogs were everywhere, tied up to their fences or porches, given little opportunity to escape the flood waters for survival. It honestly broke my heart. For a moment I thought about my girl Mandi back home and was thankful she was in the care of Dylan and Danielle.

We approached the start of our search pattern and came down to an altitude that would be well above obstacles, but low enough to spot any survivors. I opened the cabin door and sat near the edge so I could lean out and look directly below the aircraft as we flew along. My heart thumped with excitement as I expected to spot something to respond to within a matter of minutes, like all of my previous flights. We continued to fly back and forth in a series of parallel lines over the search area. My excitement began to slowly dwindle.

"This doesn't seem right," I said.

"Nope," the swimmer agreed. "It looks like the hurricane barely touched this place. It's all dry land."

He was right. We had spotted a couple of trees that fell over, but that was the extent of the damage in the area. There was no flooding and certainly no signs of distress.

"Why are we searching here?" I asked.

"We've been told to fly this search pattern," Lt Thornton said.

"Feels like we're wasting our time," Nate said. "There's still severe flooding in Beaumont."

"Let's finish the pattern. If we don't see anything, we'll refuel, say *screw it* and go to Beaumont," Lt O'Neill suggested. He was obeying a command which was our job, and we respected that. We needed to make sure nothing was overlooked.

I glanced back at the swimmer, who was nodding his head with approval. I was happy to hear the pilot say we might deviate from the established search pattern. We continued flying back and forth for another thirty minutes. I was still positioned with my head hanging out the side, scanning the ground below. I wasn't expecting to see anything, but I wasn't going to miss anything either. *God if people are in trouble, give me the eyes to find them.*

"Alright, we need some fuel guys. Let's head to Jack Brooks Regional for a top-off and then make a game plan?" LT Thornton stated.

"Let's go," Nate and I said in unison.

Jack Brooks Regional was buzzing with aircraft. Army Blackhawks, local law enforcement, and Bell 407's funneled into the runway. All of us expertly called out air traffic in all directions to deconflict a safe landing. Once on deck, we waited for our place in line to get refueled. I took this time to run into the bathroom and grab a bottle of water. The building seemed to be at max capacity. All of the drenched, exhausted yet focused aviators running around with the same goal. Rescue those in trouble.

Once up again, the weather presented an extreme challenge. Our helicopter, 6542, faced sustained tropical storm winds exceeding 35 knots with gusts over 45 knots and less than one half mile visibility. The area we were searching earlier looked fairly normal, aside from the unusual lack of human activity. Now, we were beginning to see the clear-cut evidence of Harvey's destruction. We were back in an area that was still submerged in water and had clearly been battered and beaten by the storm. We began to fly over a residential neighborhood. Like before, we flew long, parallel lines at an altitude that was as low as possible for safe flight. I could sense the energy in the cabin growing tenser, as we all knew that we were finally in an area that needed help.

"Mark, mark, mark 12 o'clock," I quickly stated.

"What do you see Ashlee?" Lt O'Neill responded.

I moved away from the cabin door and leaned between the pilots' shoulders to look forward through the cockpit windows. Just in front us, something large and white seemed to be flailing about on a balcony, but it was too far off to make out exactly what it was.

"It looks like someone is waving a flag," I said.

"Let's check it out," Nate chimed in from the back of the helicopter.

We continued our flight directly to the curious object in the distance. As we approached, we could see more clearly that a man was indeed waving a large piece of white linen from the balcony of his home. The pilot slowed down and we did a low pass over the house. As we neared the balcony, the man threw down his makeshift flag and ran to the corner of the balcony that was closest to us. He jumped onto the lower rung of the railing and leaned his whole body towards us, waving his hand frantically. He was clearly screaming though his words were inaudible, and I could clearly see a look of anguish and fear in his face.

"Alright, let's drop the swimmer and see what's going on," LT Thornton said. "This is going to be a tricky hoist." But we did it and others, just as we had done over the past four days. And after picking up a few more survivors, we took them to the closest hospital, Hermann Memorial. Then it was back out for a quick turnaround for the next hoist. We flew around for a while longer until we spotted another guy waving frantically for our attention. He also was on the balcony of his house with flood waters all around.

We came to a hover and started scanning the area for an appropriate hoist location. The flood waters were nearly at the second story of the house. The balcony where the man stood was far too small and the roof hung over it. The pilot slowly moved the helicopter to the back of the house. There was a large deck on the other side. I lowered the swimmer into an area that was safe for him to swim up to the house to investigate. He called back on the radio and reported there was a female in immediate need. She was having seizures and it was clear she was in bad shape, he relayed from his swimmer radio.

"That's going to be our only option, I think," the pilot said, referring to the large deck on the back of the house.

"I agree," I said. "But there are power lines everywhere. We're literally going to have to hoist into a box of power lines." I scanned the area a bit more. There was a line running from the roof to a pole on the right side of the deck, another line running to the neighbor's house on the left side of the deck and a main power line behind us. It would be a tricky hoist, but doable.

The man that waved us down poked his head out the door on the back deck, as if to make sure we hadn't left, and then ducked back inside. His frantic movements gave me a sense of urgency and I began to prepare the cabin to lower the swimmer.

"Ready aft for direct delivery of swimmer," I said.

I boomed the swimmer out and began to lower him. Thankfully, the winds had subsided, making it easier for the pilot to hold a steady hover and reduce the chances of swinging the swimmer into an obstacle. He descended straight down onto the deck.

"Swimmer is in the water, swimmer is disconnecting from hoist hook, hoist hook disconnected, retrieving hoist hook, clear UP AND LEFT."

I brought the hook back to the aircraft as quickly as I could and carefully watched our spacing to the power lines. The swimmer swam into the house as we continued to hover near the back deck. Less than a minute passed. The man we had seen earlier and the swimmer came rushing out the door, carrying a woman. They placed her on the deck and the swimmer threw up his hands and signaled for the rescue basket. I jumped to the back of the cabin to grab the basket and began to push it towards the cabin door.

"She's having a seizure," the LT O'Neill said. "She's having a really violent seizure."

I hooked the basket to the hoist and began to boom it out of the cabin. As I started to lower the basket towards the deck, I got a look at the survivor. Her body was jerking and thrashing about. I placed the basket in the water just a few feet from the swimmer who was holding her. Putting her in the basket was no easy task. As they tried to ease her towards the basket, her flailing limbs would kick the basket away. They were finally able to get her legs and torso into the basket and the swimmer gave me a thumbs up.

"Survivor is ready for pick up," I said. "Prepare to take the load. Taking the load…" I gently eased the basket out of the water while the swimmer steadied the basket from below. "Survivor is clear of the water. Survivor is five feet off up…"

Just then the man still on the porch threw a huge bag of the woman's medicine to Nate, who immediately motioned for me to lower the woman back down so he could add her bag to the basket. I continued to hoist the survivor towards the helicopter. I was hoisting her a bit slower than normal, as I carefully eyed the obstacles surrounding the house. There was a *huge* tree just feet from me and I wanted to ensure my basket didn't make contact. The basket was steady beneath the helicopter. It wasn't swinging but the woman was convulsing so violently that I thought at any moment she was going to seizure right out.

"I can feel her convulsing," the LT O'Neill explained. "It's so bad that I can feel it in the controls."

The woman was jerking and thrashing so violently that the effects could be felt in the helicopter. I was so preoccupied with the dangers of the power lines, that I had not considered the danger of her convulsing out of the basket. I continued to hoist her towards the helicopter.

"Survivor is ten feet off the deck…"

She was now out of the reach of the rescue swimmer and completely in my hands. I continued to raise her towards the helicopter. My eyes continued darting to the power lines, trees, and then back to her thrashing body.

"Survivor is..."

My chin suddenly sunk to my chest and I found myself staring at the floor of the cabin. I tried to raise my head to look back at the basket, but the strength to do so was completely lost. I quickly stopped hoisting the woman. I didn't want to move her without being able to see what I was doing.

"Ashlee, what's going on? Keep talking to us!" LT O'Neill said. Not only did I just feel all strength leave my body, it was as if my energy seemed to have evaporated in an instant. In sheer panic, I tried desperately to use the muscles in my neck to hold my head up but found myself incapable of commanding my own body. My heart raced as I began to realize the severity of the situation. *What is happening to my body?!*

The woman continued to experience serious convulsions as she dangled precariously from a helicopter in a basket that was rocking to and fro near power lines. I forced my eyes to maintain focus on her but I was so terrified that she was going to seize out of the basket. All the while my body felt as though someone pressed an *off* button and my internal batteries had died.

"Ashlee, breathe," the LT O'Neill exclaimed. "You are doing great. I have a steady hover!" clearly sensing something was wrong. Using the strength still left in my arms, I pulled my head up with my hand and managed to put eyes on the survivor.

"Survivor is halfway up. Altitude and position are good..." *Jesus help me. Jesus help me,* I kept repeating over and over in my head, *Please give me the strength...*" I was truly terrified. I mustered every ounce of strength and it seemed as though my prayers had been answered. "Bringing up survivor," I said. "Survivor is ten feet below the aircraft. Survivor is five feet below the aircraft. Survivor is at the door. Booming in survivor..." I repeated, "Booming in survivor."

I tugged on the basket to bring this lady in, but her arms and legs were so rigid it made this evolution difficult. Once the hoist was fully boomed in, I took a deep breath and used every last ounce of strength I could muster to pull her into the cabin, still in the rescue basket, as I gave slack on the hoist cable. As I pulled, I could feel the rest of my muscles start shutting down. The basket felt twenty times heavier than it ever had before, but I was refused to quit. I kept pulling with what little strength my body could summon. Finally, with sweat rolling down my face, I got her far enough into the cabin to disconnect the hoist hook.

"Survivor is in the cabin. Hoist hook disconnected." I took in a huge breath of air and exhaled with an open mouth. "Thank you, Jesus," I said under my breath. In my heart, I knew He gave me that last ounce of strength that I needed to finish my job.

We were able to land at Hermann Memorial helo pad where Nate and I carried the rescue basket to the awaiting hospital staff to transfer to the gurney. We were bagged out after that flight. I was grateful for that, it meant I wouldn't have to voluntarily pull myself from future flights, forcing me to explain my situation. I needed time to process the events of the last hour before trying to explain it to anyone else. I wasn't going to fly anymore knowing how I felt.

All I knew was that my body failed. My body failed when someone else's life was in my hands. It was with my final hoist in hurricane Harvey that I knew something was horribly wrong with me and that an important chapter of my life was about to come to a close.

Our last day of flying. Left to right, AST3 Nate Feske-Wood, LTJG Ryan O'Neill, and me.

[18] ONE MORE RESCUE

"She was afraid of heights,
but she was much more afraid of never flying."

—Atticus

THE NEXT DAY, crews from other air stations began slowly making their way home. After helping complete maintenance in the morning, I was informed that I would be heading home as well, and I couldn't have been more relieved. After we loaded our gear and headed toward New Orleans my eyes looked at the scenes passing below. The normalcy regained the more east we traveled. Children playing in backyards, dogs being walked through neighborhoods, and lawn mowers releasing the fresh smell of summer into the air. This was a stark difference from the complete devastation I had just witnessed. *Wow,* I thought to myself. It almost seemed as though the rest of the world hadn't a clue. I examined my flight suit only to notice seems bursting and rips from the days prior. My tired eyes soon turned heavy and sleep welcomed me. Once our flight landed back at NAS JRB New Orleans, I bid a safe farewell to my crew, and we were told to go home to take a few days to *decompress*.

I walked to my car eager to pick up my Mandi girl from the Hernandez's house, get a bottle of wine, and sit in my bath tub in silence. My thoughts trailed off as I drove off base: *I wonder how my Mandi pants has been. What kind of wine am I going to buy? Crap, I hope my plants aren't dead. Jeez, I can't ever keep those alive.* And just as I felt the decompression begin and a tinge of normalcy return to my life, *BOOM! CRASH!*

Right in front of me there was a violent collision between two vehicles. Instantly I was thrashed back into first responder mode. I parked my vehicle to call 911 and assess the survivors. As I was calling 911, I walked up to the driver-side door. There was an elderly man with his bloody face resting on the air bag. His seat was pushed all the way back. I asked him to remain still and that help was on the way. After relaying the location to police I quickly hung up and checked the stability of the man. He was dazed and startled, but in stable condition. I asked him to remain still as to not exacerbate any possible injuries and continued to comfort him. I walked over to the second vehicle and this man was out and walking about. Once the ambulance and police arrived, they cleared me to go ahead and leave, and that everything was under control.

Once I drove away, the emotion overwhelmed me. I broke down and started uncontrollably sobbing. This was a pivotal moment for me. Every bit of compartmentalizing I had done was slowly unraveling. I called Bob Hovey on my speed dial. He was my rescue swimmer in the first crew out to Houston. He would get it. I don't even remember what I said but Bob gave me the comforting words that I needed at the time. Once I got Mandi, I went home and enjoyed the silence I had been craving for days. My mind was riddled with helicopter noise. I needed silence. Once in the bath with a glass of wine, the tears began, and didn't stop for hours.

Epilogue

Diagnosis and State of the Union

THE AFTERMATH of my personal experience with Hurricane Harvey came with some of the highest highs and lowest lows of my life. My first priority upon returning to New Orleans was my own health. My symptoms could no longer be brushed off. My last hoist was nearly devastating and a clear indication that I was suffering from a condition far more serious than all of the doctors seemed to think. I talked to the flight surgeon about my last hoist and described how terrifying it was to lose control of my muscles. He referred me to a neurologist. Unlike all of the doctors I had seen before, the neurologist didn't seem confused or appear to be guessing when he decided how to proceed with my care. He immediately ordered a blood panel.

I fully expected to wait weeks to hear back about the blood panel, but his office called me the very next day. The lady on the phone told me I needed to come in and talk to the doctor about my results. As soon as she said this, I knew they had found something. Bad news is always given in person.

I went in to see the doctor. I wasn't actually scheduled for an appointment, so I ended up sitting in the waiting room for several hours. The time spent waiting made me more and more anxious. I sat there thinking about the endless hours of researching my symptoms on the internet and trying to figure out which one I might have. I thought about how each disease might impact my future in different ways. I thought about my own mortality as I considered the very real possibility that my own quality or length of life could become significantly reduced. Only a few days prior, I was prepared to lay down my own life in the middle of a hurricane to save the life of another, and now here I was back in the safety of dry land but fearing for my future.

The contrast seemed so strange.

I was called in and the doctor motioned for me to sit on the other side of his desk. He weaved his fingers together, placed his hands on his desk and leaned forward a bit.

"You have myasthenia gravis," he said. I heard his words but I was having trouble processing them. I knew I had read about this disease at some point but I couldn't recall anything about it. I continued to stare straight ahead, my hands trembling slightly. "It's an autoimmune disease. Basically, there are antibodies that are either blocking or destroying receptors at the junction between the nerve and muscle. This stops nerve pulses from triggering muscle contractions, which is why you've been experiencing loss of muscle control."

The words *autoimmune disease* hit me like a bombshell. This was the sort of thing you see happen to other people, but never expect to happen to yourself.

"Is it going to get worse?" I asked.

"I'm going to put you on a medication that you will have to take four times a day. This should increase your muscle control and help with the general fatigue you've been experiencing. Most people live out a relatively normal life as long as they take their medicine. But, it's important that you know that you will be living with this condition for the rest of your life. There is always a chance that your condition could degrade, even with the medicine. It's just something you're going to have to monitor."

I looked down at my hands and allowed myself a moment to take in the news. The shaking in my fingers subsided and the anxiety I'd felt in the waiting room had left me.

"How do you feel about all this?" the doctor asked.

"I'm glad I'm not crazy," I said. "I thought I was losing my mind. I had been trying to figure out what was wrong with me for years and every doctor I saw kind of dismissed me."

I felt relieved.

It was an odd reaction to life changing news, but I felt like a massive weight had been lifted off my shoulders. There would be no more late-night Google searches, no more playing musical doctors, and no more questioning my own sanity.

I left the doctor's office. I felt more peace in that moment then I had in years. But slowly, concerns about how my future could be affected by this disease started to take over. Naturally I was scared, but I felt confident facing whatever difficulties may come because I was finally armed with an understanding of my condition.

It was no surprise that when my flight surgeon learned of my diagnosis, he grounded me and we discussed my options for my career. Flying had been such a huge part of my life and one of my greatest passions for well over a decade, and if I couldn't fly then this job wasn't for me. In many ways, it defined me. I struggled with my identity more than anything in the months following my diagnosis.

I continued to work at the air station. While I couldn't fly, I found plenty of ways to make myself useful. I became the training petty officer, which was a tedious desk job. It required running report after report, tracking the minimum of every enlisted member, and other various odd jobs. Staying busy kept my mind engaged. This helped me stay calm as I muddled my way through the process of getting medically discharged.

Shortly after my diagnosis, while at work one day, I received a phone call from a blocked number. I don't answer calls from numbers I don't know, so I ignored it. Minutes later, I received another call from a blocked number. I stared at my phone for a moment. Curiosity got the best of me and I answered the call.

"Hello?" I said.

"Hello. Is this Petty Officer Second Class Leppert?" a woman's voice asked.

"Yes, may I ask who's calling?"

"Yes. This is Jess Walker calling from the White House, The President and First Lady would like to formally invite you to the State of the Union Address," she said. This caught me completely off guard. I couldn't find the words to respond. After a slightly awkward pause, she continued, and told me that someone would be in touch with me to plan travel and lodging. I was already struggling to process the events of the hurricane, the shock of my diagnosis, and the impending medical discharge, so this unexpected yet welcomed invitation was a great distraction.

In attending the State of the Union Address, I went from experiencing one of the lowest points in my life, to one of the highest. While I expected to be seated somewhere in the back row where I could easily see the President, I did not expect to be seated directly next to the Second Lady, Karen Pence, and I did not expect the President to personally identify me during his speech and make mention of my crew's work during Hurricane Harvey. As someone with an outgoing personality, I don't normally have a problem with having some attention on me, but being recognized by the President, and all the important figureheads around me, left me completely speechless and humbled.

Me, seated, at the State of the Union Address receiving a standing ovation while representing the entire Coast Guard's efforts during the devastating Hurricane Harvey, January 30, 2018.

Image © White House Photo by Andrea Hanks

After the conclusion of the State of the Union Address, I was able to take pictures with President Trump in the Oval Office. I had personal, one-on-one conversations with the first and second ladies and took a selfie with Vice President Pence, at his request! What an honor. I was even able to bring my rescue swimmer from my first crew, Bob Hovey as my "plus one." I couldn't think of a better way to bring closure to my career in the U.S. Coast Guard.

THE HURRICANE WITHIN

In the Oval Office! From left to right, Bob Hovey, President Donald Trump, me. Image © White House Photo by Shealah Craighead

After the hurricane rescues it seemed as though the flood gates to my soul opened. I began not only having PTSD from this terrifying event but nightmares as well. At times I wished I could go back and hug 19-year-old Ashlee, and just tell her that it wasn't her fault. But from that trauma I became stronger. Unbreakable, even. The natural emotional and spiritual power I found in seeking healing through God is what gave me the backbone to face every other negative life event thereafter.

One thing has remained true throughout my entire life, and that's the *peace* that the promises of God has given me. From growing up surrounded by addicts, to surviving a sexual assault, battling an auto-immune disease, and with my crews safely rescuing over 49 people during the scariest five days of my life, the truth remains that the power of perseverance and strength stems from the Lord.

I'm still working through the medical discharge process as I conclude this memoir. I still haven't quite figured out where I will be heading, or what I will be doing. I would like to travel the United States and speak to people about my experiences, myasthenia gravis, and managing PTSD. I'm still a bit anxious, but my reflection on the events of Hurricane Harvey and my disease have given me a great deal of insight, making the future look more exciting than terrifying. I now know I have the strength to weather any storm life decides to throw at me. And in those moments I need a little extra help, I know without any doubt that God will be there to see me through. Our trials can be overcome with the Lord Jesus on our side. He did have *something bigger* in store for me, and He in all of this has given me something to leave you with to help you through as well.

Give it all to God. Let Him help you overcome your own hurricane within.

Ms. Mandi Pants (the star of my book lol) and me, March, 2019.

Ashlee Leppert

THE WHITE HOUSE
WASHINGTON

February 28, 2018

Petty Officer Second Class Ashlee Leppert, USCG
New Orleans, Louisiana

Dear Petty Officer Leppert,

Thank you for being our guest at the State of the Union Address. It was truly an honor to have you in attendance.

We were proud to share with the country your heroic efforts during the devastating hurricanes. Our Nation and our very way of life endure because selfless service members like you demonstrate unwavering courage and resolve in times of dire need.

America honors you, and we are grateful for your service. We send our best wishes to you and your family for good health, happiness, and prosperity.

Sincerely,

THE HURRICANE WITHIN

AFTERWORD

REMEMBERING HURRICANE KATRINA

The story below is an intimate account of Hurricane Katrina behind the eyes of John Jamison. He shares some of his personal accounts of a devastating time for the city of New Orleans. Thank you John and the rest of the crews for giving us a glimpse into this tragedy. Your heroic actions shined hope into so many lives. —Ashlee

I TRANSFERRED into New Orleans in the summer of 2005. It was hot, sticky, and flat compared to the mountainous coast of Northern California I had just left. I settled into the fast-paced routine quickly which was a welcome change from the sleepy air station where I had just served. About one month after my arrival, my chief was strolling through the shop looking for names for "fly away crews." He asked me if I was willing to crew an open spot, to which I replied, "sure." After agreeing to go, I had to ask, "What is a fly away crew?" He chuckled and informed me that there was a hurricane moving through the Caribbean gaining strength, and should that storm track towards New Orleans, we would evacuate the five helicopters and respond to the city in the wake of its path. About three or four days later I reported to the air station for duty and found it to be a ghost town. As I walked into our maintenance control—the brains of the day-to-day operations—I found about eight Coasties on phones, all talking at once. The weather channel was on and the screen showed a monstrous spinning mass in the Gulf of Mexico.

The scene was like something out of a movie—I was surprised there were not red phones on the countertop with direct lines to the president. I was told to go home, pack and return the following morning. We were evacuating the unit. I returned the following morning after a night of pre-hurricane merriment and well wishes from the locals in Algiers Point. We promptly got the helicopters out of the hangar and made our way to Lake Charles, LA, which is a great place to be from. I shared a room with AET2 Roberto Lopez. We tried our best to go to sleep that night but it was a fitful rest at best.

When we woke in the morning, the red monster on the TV had grown larger and angrier, we knew what was in store for us. We had an amazing continental breakfast at the Microtel, complete with individually-wrapped cheese Danishes and what was heralded as "gourmet coffee blend." We were too excited to eat much else. Our five aircrews made our way to the hangar and proceeded with the pre-flight inspections in nervous anticipation. The weather in Lake Charles was blustery and warm. We took off without incident and made our way to the crescent city. As we went we flew in loose formation. Buffeted by the winds I watched the helicopter in front of me rise and fall rapidly with massive gusts of wind blowing all of us around. We all landed just southwest of the city to re-group and discuss our plan of attack. Our pilots quickly broke the city into sections and we set about to provide damage assessments and reports to the authorities on response. What we found was astonishing.

The winds and storm swell had taken a considerable toll on the city and surrounding areas but the worst was yet to come. My crew was tasked with the lakeside area of the city. As we orbited we began to see people who were stranded with water quickly rising from levees that recently broke open. The scene was like something out of a Michael Bay film—the *water was on fire*! We set about the task of picking people up and simply moving them to higher ground. Soon after picking up a few survivors, we noticed other survivors waving out of the eaves of their roofs, the water had risen to the roof tops. In a moment of ingenuity, my crew placed our rescue swimmer on one roof to communicate with the survivors, and in the cabin of our aircraft we discussed possible strategies for exfiltration of the family from the attic. Ultimately we lowered our aircraft's crash axe (an axe designed to penetrate the thin aluminum skin of an aircraft, not wood and asphalt shingles) to our rescue swimmer. He quickly began hacking at the home's roof.

We proceeded to complete rescues until we hit our *bag limits* (the amount of time which we could safely stay airborne). However, our last evolution involved a daring rescue of a man who looked identical to the skipper from Gilligan's Island, a fact made more ironic given the barrel-chested nature of the man and his miniature companion which happened to be a Chihuahua. We recovered his companion from a rooftop and commenced the evolution to recover Skipper. Once in the basket I began bringing him up, keeping my pilot informed of all that was going on below the aircraft. It was dark now, the city had little electricity, so what is normally a well-lit suburban area was only visible through the pilot's landing lights, add the fact that we were in a low hover surrounded by enormous live oaks and power lines. As Skipper began to come away from the rooftop in the basket, I noticed the pilot began to transition the aircraft forward.

In a normal hoist evolution the aircraft remains stationary while the device (the basket) and the survivor are brought straight up into the cabin of the helicopter. However, the Skipper was so heavy that as we began to pick him up the helicopter began to struggle under the additional weight. This drives the pilot's need for airspeed to provide additional lift. As we transitioned forward I told the pilot to "hold his position."

"I can't," he replied, "he's too heavy, he'll pull us into the drink."

The aircraft began a slow transition forward as I pulled the giant man upwards. It seemed as though the basket barely cleared the power lines—but of course, this could be 15 years of history making my own memories into legend. We landed at the Superdome to off-load our passengers and it was at this point my crew found levity in the situation. The pilots wanted to have a look at the "man who almost pulled us into the drink." The laughter began as we saw the contrast between him and his chihuahua. We joked that it wasn't the man, but the dog who made us heavy.

When we landed that night, sweat-drenched and weary both mentally and physically, we went to sleep on office and conference room floors. The next morning brought an awesome display of Coast Guard aviation as I awoke to what looked like an airshow. There were numerous types of aircraft and more orange MH-65 helicopters than I had ever seen before. It was a chaotic symphony of turning helicopters and people. At times, survivors showed up at our air station. Other times, it was rescue dogs that compassionate aircrews refused to leave behind. There was a time many of us had rescue dogs living in our FEMA trailers until we could find them proper homes. At this point in my life, those days all blur into one amazing event populated by sadness, desperation, laughter, and camaraderie. It was an unprecedented response to the Gulf Coast disaster, one which I thought I would never see again. Boy was I wrong.

Fast forward to about 12 years later and I find myself stationed once again at the busiest single airframe unit in the Coast Guard—Air Station New Orleans. I returned to the unit in May of 2017, this time as a Chief Petty Officer with a different role and responsibility. When Hurricane Harvey was making its way to Corpus Christie, Texas, I was selected to lead a maintenance crew to the area in support of the helicopters being dispatched from New Orleans. We headed straight to Houston in an effort to pre-stage our support for the helo and its crew. If you're reading this book, you are aware of what occurred next.

I do not wish to tell my tale of Houston here, I will happily leave that to Ashlee and the brave aircrews who flew into some of the scariest conditions I have witnessed in 20 years of Coast Guard aviation. I will say this—it was a joy, and certainly divine timing, to be a support to those men and women who were doing similar, and oftentimes more harrowing rescues than I did only 12 years before. It was an honor to serve them as a leader, to make sure they were taken care of and stood up for. For both storms, it was heartbreaking for those who lost homes and family members. For those of us living in the city of New Orleans and Houston, we empathized with them, as many Coasties dealt with similar plights. But for the few of us who got the opportunity to rescue those cities, it was simply amazing. It was the reason we signed up for this job—the desire to save lives, to help when help seemed impossible.

For all of this I am grateful.

John Jamison

USCG Chief Petty Officer

About the Author

ASHLEE LEPPERT is a veteran of the United States Coast Guard where she proudly served as a helicopter mechanic and rescue flight crew member. She enjoyed the distinct honor of receiving a personal invitation to President Trump's 2018 State of the Union Address. There, Ashlee was addressed directly by the President and commended, on behalf of her and her crew, for their rescue work during the devastating Hurricane Harvey.

Ashlee overcame hardships and met challenges with grace under the guidance of God. "I have come away with valuable lessons to share," she says. "Life's challenges have taught me to be not just a survivor, but someone who thrives in this amazing, beautiful, complicated world. Today, it is my passion to share my unique story through my inspirational speaking engagements."

Please visit AshleeLeppert.com to learn more or inquire about booking Ashlee to spark inspiration at your next event.

Speaking

Hire Me to Inspire Your Group!

TODAY, IT IS MY PASSION to share my unique story through my inspirational speaking engagements."

Scan the QR code below and visit AshleeLeppert.com to learn more or inquire about booking Ashlee to spark inspiration at your next event.

Ms. Ashlee Leppert graciously agreed to speak and the result was a standing ovation from that audience. Her presentation was polished and engaging. Her adventures in performing her duties were remarkable and captivating. Her confident, inspirational performance in front of the audience created exactly the atmosphere I was hoping for and her story touched our hearts as well. I greatly recommend her.

—Kim M. Wintner, Col. USAF (ret.)

ACKNOWLEDGEMENTS

THROUGHOUT MY LIFE, there have been so many significant, impactful people who have made such a positive difference in how I live my life. So many mentors have carved my path to success and have shown me how to be a great leader all the while staying true to my personal values and myself. My family—Coast Guard and blood related—have watched me over the years go through some extreme highs and lows. I am forever grateful for all of the Coast Guard members that I have had the privilege to serve this great nation with, from my days at boot camp, to my wild child non-rate days in Puerto Rico and Elizabeth City, NC, through my early aviation career in Detroit, and finally ending with New Orleans. The memories I have will be a constant reminder of how proud I was to wear the uniform of the world's best Coast Guard.

A huge thank you to those friends and family who given me unwavering support at times in the face of great adversity. My *ride-or-die* Michigan family and friends, *thank you*. You all truly have been a constant form of support no matter the distance between us. I love you all more than words can say.

Your prayers for my safety and the safety of my crews were heard and delivered and I am alive today by the grace of God.

Thank you Mom and Dad for instilling the confidence and determined mindset to never give up and fight for what I want out of life.

Thank you Marrero CrossFit members and coaches for helping me recharge my mental and physical health. You all inspire me and push me to be a better version of myself even when I thought I couldn't do it.

This goes without saying, but there are not enough *thank you's* I could say to my crews and co-workers from Hurricane Harvey. We know that the mission is never accomplished by one person. My pilots, rescue swimmers, fellow hanger deck wrench turners, and the logistical brains behind the curtain all played a crucial part in getting the mission done and making sure those aircraft returned home safely. Thank you. May God continue to bless you all with a lifetime of happiness and success.

Thank you Katherine O'Nale, my amazing friend for over 10 years. Katherine and I met in Avionics Electrical Technician School. We instantly became best friends despite being very opposite in many aspects of life and looks. Our common bond of a love of aviation and a good laugh solidified our friendship for life. Thank you a million times over for helping me tell my story.

Thank you to AST3 Ethan McKenzie for being the first person to help me organize my chaotic memories from my Hurricane Harvey rescues. Your expert writing skills helped me initially preserve my thoughts from those hectic moments and ultimately laid an amazing foundation for this story.

To all of my doctors, thank you for doing your best and most professional job at helping me get a diagnosis. Pinpointing an autoimmune disease, with extremely intermittent symptoms, is extremely challenging. I appreciate your expertise and patience with me as I struggled to figure out what was wrong. God Bless you all.

This is my story alone. I am not trying to portray the Coast Guard or the job of being a flight mechanic in any other perspective than my own. The stories you will read about are all recalled to the best of my ability. The wonderful people whom I speak about have agreed to be a part of my story. I hope you enjoy this story and the amazing acts of heroism in it. I have had the utmost privilege working and flying alongside some of the best the country has to offer. It has truly been an honor.

The anchor for my life is my Lord and Savior Jesus Christ. He alone fills my life with hope and happiness. May this book bring all the Glory to God and speak of His great promises.

LEARN MORE

HERE ARE SOME worthy causes and resources I'd like to share:

Myasthenia Gravis Foundation of America

https://myasthenia.org/

Hurricane Preparedness

https://www.nhc.noaa.gov/prepare/ready.php

PTSD Awareness

https://www.ptsd.va.gov/understand/awareness/index.asp

Veteran Suicide Crisis Hotline

https://www.veteranscrisisline.net/

Want to learn more about the Coast Guard?

https://www.gocoastguard.com/

The Hurricane Within

Praise Jesus Vintage New Orleans Style

http://www.vintagechurchnola.com

Visit my website for more resources, pictures, and booking opportunities!

http://www.thehurricanewithin.com